THE WILD
Hayling Island

Pete Durnell
John Walters

Cover photographs:
Dunlin (Simon Colenutt)
Adder (Simon Colenutt)
Painted Lady (Pete Durnell)
Brent Geese (Dennis Johnson)
Sea Holly at Black Point (Pete Durnell)

*Dedicated to my parents Ann and Stan
who gave me this wonderful hobby.*

PRD

ISBN 0-9540256-0-1

Printed by Wotton Printers Ltd, Newton Abbot (01626) 353698

Contents

Foreword

It is a great pleasure for me to write a foreword for this book.

As pointed out in our *Flora of Hampshire* (with Lady Anne Brewis and Paul Bowman) the south-east corner of Hampshire is not only the most densely populated area of its coastline, with massive residential, industrial and Ministry of Defence development, but has, paradoxically, the richest diversity of coastal habitats.

It is quite remarkable how much has survived by way of rich plant communities, rare plants, birds and invertebrates. It must have been vastly richer 200 years and more ago, when most of our coastline was an undeveloped wilderness; I would myself much like to have seen it at that time!

What survives, and is described in this book is a remarkable tribute not only to nature, but to the efforts made by enthusiastic conservationists, including not only the keen amateurs but also the local authorities (Hampshire County Council and Havant Borough Council) who have gone to so much trouble and expense to conserve what they can of this splendid coastal area.

Even within the built-up parts of the coastline, many fine habitats survive (quite remarkably) between the houses and the sea shore itself on remnants of the formerly extensive commons of Hayling.

This delightful book about Hayling is wonderfully comprehensive, starting with an excellent geological and historical introduction, it covers all groups of plants and animals that occur there, and dicusses their habitats.

The authors are to be warmly congratulated on this book. It is beautifully illustrated in colour and provides an example of what can be done by way of a study of a small area, but is rarely attempted, at least not with as much success as has been done here.

Every resident and serious-minded visitor to Hayling should obtain this book, whether they are naturalists or not. It is packed with valuable and interesting information in its small compass, much of it that would otherwise be difficult to obtain. It is a must for every resident and serious visitor with any interest in the environment.

Francis Rose

Dr Francis Rose, MBE - joint author of the *Flora of Hampshire* and formerly Reader in Biogeography, King's College, London.

Hayling Island
Wildlife Habitats

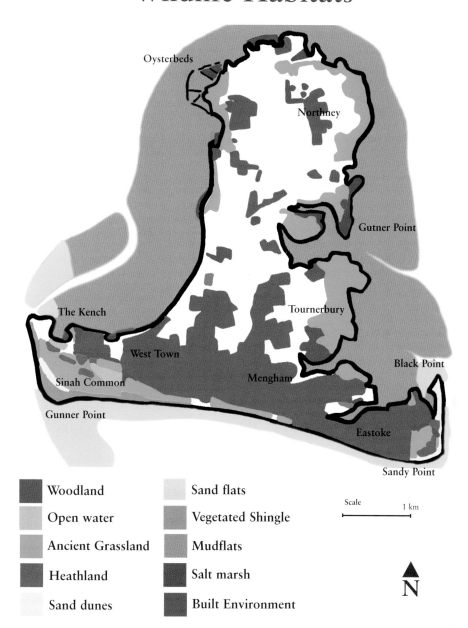

Oysterbeds

Northney

Gutner Point

The Kench

Tournerbury

West Town

Black Point

Sinah Common

Mengham

Gunner Point

Eastoke

Sandy Point

Woodland

Sand flats

Open water

Vegetated Shingle

Ancient Grassland

Mudflats

Heathland

Salt marsh

Sand dunes

Built Environment

Scale

1 km

N

Introduction

'Hayling Island possess every requisite advantage in a singularly eminent degree; her shores are washed by the ocean pure and uncontaminated by other waters; her fields are fertile; and the views at her command are of that variety and pleasing character which every admirer of nature is fond of contemplating.'

From a Topographical and Historical Account of Hayling Island (1826).

Much has changed on the island since these words were written, but Hayling is still graced with a wonderful diversity of wildlife. On still winter nights, the calls of Brent Geese and waders carry across Hayling's marshes as they have for centuries.

Amidst modern development and tourism, Hayling has retained extensive salt marshes, mudflats, remnants of heathland, flower-rich meadows and sand dunes. The vegetated shingle beach at Gunner Point is one of the prime areas in Hampshire for coastal plants.

Situated in the middle of one of the most important wetland areas in Britain, Hayling has been known to naturalists and hunters for centuries. Despite this interest in the island no previous attempt has been made to draw together its varied wildlife in a single account.

Much of Hayling's most interesting and distinctive wildlife is found in the harbours and waters which surround it. For the purposes of this book, and to make it of more practical use, we have decided to stretch the island's boundaries a little, to include those species which can be seen from its shores as well as on land.

Our aim in writing this book is to share some of the experiences and insights we have gained while living and working on Hayling and hopefully to increase awareness of the island's natural riches. The book does not attempt a comprehensive coverage of all aspects of the island's natural history but is intended to highlight those things which make Hayling so special.

We have set out to answer some of the most frequently asked questions concerning the island's wildlife and to provide some guidance on the best places to see it.

The book is arranged in chapters, each looking at a different habitat and its associated wildlife. There are sections on the formation of the island and the background to its current natural history. We also look at conservation on Hayling and attempt to predict what the future might hold for its wildlife. Finally we have included a month-by-month guide giving ideas of the best places to observe many of the species described in the book.

Geology and History

To understand and appreciate the wildlife of Hayling it is useful to look at the natural forces which have shaped the geology of the island. The interactions between geology and man over thousands of years have resulted in the landscape and wildlife we see today.

The making of an island

During the last Ice Age around 20,000 years ago, vast quantities of water were locked up in the polar ice caps, causing sea levels around the world to be approximately 100 metres lower than they are today. Between what is now Britain and France lay a broad flat plain across which ran a large river system taking meltwater from southern England. The 'Solent River', as it is now known, flowed between Hampshire and the Isle of Wight with several tributaries entering it from higher ground to the north, now Portsdown Hill. Most of the mud, sand and gravel which form the island today was brought down these huge prehistoric rivers or carried on strong icy winds.

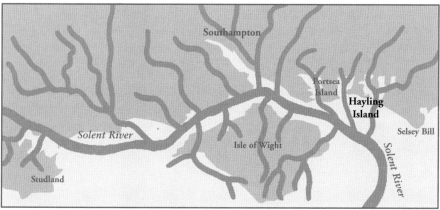

At the end of the last Ice Age large tributaries carrying meltwater from high ground flowed down into the Solent River. These tributaries flowed either side of the formative Portsea and Hayling Islands.

As the climate warmed and the ice melted, sea levels rose, cutting Britain off from the continent and gradually drowning the upper reaches of these tributaries, forming what are now the harbours of Portsmouth, Langstone and Chichester. Until recently it was thought the harbours were flooded between 9000 and 5000 years ago, effectively forming Hayling into an island. Recent archaeological finds in Langstone Harbour appear to show that much of the harbour was still wooded only 2000 years ago. A mixture of willow and **Alder** grew in a low-lying depression, periodically flooded by the rivers flowing from the north. The exact date when rising sea levels pushed sea-water into the harbours is not known. It may well be that the Romans did not see Hayling as an island, but as part of a low-lying coastal plain.

Geology

The geology of Hayling is varied with the northern two-thirds of the island mainly 'Brickearth' (fertile brown soil) over a base of chalk, the middle is brickearth over clay and the southern coastal strip made up of sand and gravel.

Climate

The moderating effect of the surrounding sea, which acts like a giant storage heater, gives Hayling an extremely mild climate with few days of hard frost. Being on the south coast, the island also enjoys high temperatures and levels of sunshine. Rainfall is relatively low at around 800 mm per year. The combination of climatic factors has been important in the development of the island's wildlife, enabling essentially continental species to survive on the northern edge of their ranges.

Hayling's wildlife before man

Around 15,000 years ago the vegetation of early Hayling began a series of transformations as the climate became milder. The initial windblown tundra-type landscape with lichens and sedges would gradually have given way to grasses and hardy wildflowers such as saxifrages. Later, pioneer trees such as **Birch**, willow and **Scots Pine** would have started to appear. This early colonising forest slowly became mature woodland as more tree species including **Oak** and **Ash** arrived from the south. Finally, around 8,500 years ago, Britain was cut off from the rest of Europe and no more species could arrive naturally*.

Much of southern England including Hayling Island was at this time largely covered by dense 'wildwood'. This was very unlike today's woodlands. Some tree species, such as **Small-leaved Lime** which are currently rare, were then abundant, alongside **Elm**, **Hazel** and Alder. Familiar trees today, such as **Sycamore**, **Sweet** and **Horse Chestnut** would have been absent as they have been introduced to this country by man.

At the wildwood's greatest extent, trees grew almost everywhere except on coastal sand dunes and salt marshes, where low fertility and salt water would have kept them at bay. The forests contained many large herbivores which maintained open glades by heavy grazing and trampling. In these, sometimes extensive open areas, the ancestors of our many grassland and heathland plants and animals must have lived.

* Only 2000 of approximately 5000 species of plant on the nearby continent made it across before the waters rose. This is the reason why Britain has an impoverished flora compared to continental Europe.

The mammals which roamed these forests were very different from today's inhabitants. Our familiar Foxes would have had to share the land with **Wild Boar, Roe** and **Red Deer, Wolves, Auroch** (a large, now extinct, cow) and possibly even **Brown Bear.** In the treetops, **Red Squirrels**, not the introduced **Grey Squirrel,** may have been hunted by **Pine Martens.** The roots of large waterside trees may have made ideal sites for **Otter** holts and many species of bat would have lived in the mature forest. Woodland birds such as woodpeckers and **Nuthatches** must have been far commoner than they are today, while familiar species of open country, such as **Skylarks** and **Meadow Pipits,** would have been confined to the open glades.

We can only speculate how Hayling must have appeared to its first human inhabitants and guess as to which species they encountered. What is certain is that the arrival of man eventually led to profound changes for the wildlife which lived there.

The arrival of man

The discovery of 10,000 year old stone tools in Langstone Harbour indicates that Stone Age man probably lived on Hayling, hunting the abundant deer and Wild Boar in the forests. A Wild Boar tusk recently found in the garden of Mengham House may well have been left by these nomadic hunters.

Despite his long occupation of Hayling, Stone Age man did little to modify the wooded landscape. It was the arrival in Britain of farming from the Middle East which was to make a dramatic and lasting impression on Hayling and its wildlife.

Bronze Age man (2600 BC - 750 BC) lived chiefly on the high ground of the chalk downs where the forest cover was thinner and it was easier to move about and to clear areas for sheep grazing. Much of Hampshire's chalk downland was cleared of trees 5000 years ago and has remained so ever since. The thickly wooded coastal lowlands such as Hayling Island retained their tree cover far longer but, by 1000 BC, man was starting to create clearings in this coastal forest too.

Iron Age (750 BC - AD 43) remains have been found at Tournerbury. These people kept cattle, sheep and pigs and practised an early form of arable farming. Now able to use hard metal axes, Iron Age man felled most of

Hayling's remaining forests to accommodate a growing population. In addition to clearing the forest, hunting pressure led to the extinction of Wild Boar and the extermination of the Wolf to protect domestic stock. Patterns of woodland clearance at this time still have an echo in the landscape today. Some woodland, mainly on less fertile soils, was retained and managed to produce timber, firewood and coppice materials. The Forest of Bere between Fareham and Havant is one such area with a long history of woodland management.

On Hayling, it appears that the soil, especially the Brickearth in the north of the island was so fertile that the land was rapidly cleared for agriculture. In central Hayling however, the Brickearth lies over clay, making it heavy to work and frequently waterlogged. This central strip remained tree-covered long after the rest of the island had been cleared, dividing the island into two communities, north and south of the wood. Even as late as the 20th century large areas of woodland survived in central Hayling.

By Roman times the majority of Hayling was being used for arable production. So favourable were the conditions that surplus corn was exported to France. Only the infertile sand and gravel strip along the south coast of the island remained uncultivated, but was grazed by livestock.

By 1086, Hayling was the most densely-populated area around Chichester Harbour. This comprised some 94 households with a population of 420, four times the number of people then living on Portsea island! The isolated nature of the island meant that this situation remained static and, by 1801, over 700 years later, the population had grown to just 578 individuals.

The people of Hayling were still largely an agricultural community with some fishing, salt and brick-making. Much of the island was still open common until the *Acts of Enclosure* in 1840. By 1876, apart from the Beachlands area, all Hayling's commons had been enclosed and the pace of agricultural reform began to speed up.

Today the island is largely a mixture of urban development and farmland. Despite 20th century pressures, Hayling still retains a range of habitats which have somehow survived in hidden corners often due to accidents of history and their unsuitability for agriculture.

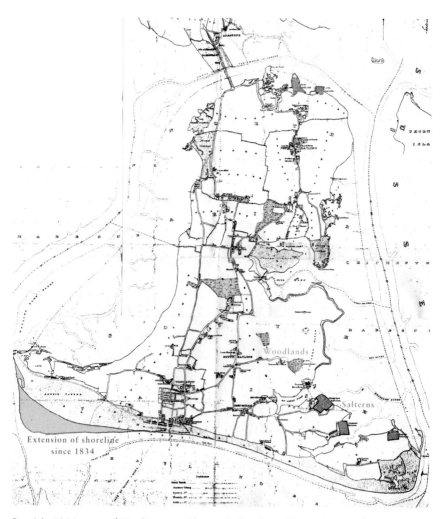

Lewis's 1834 map of Hayling provides an indication of how the island appeared at the time. The southern coastal strip consists of open common land, a large rabbit warren at Sinah with Gunner Point far smaller than it is today.

At Sandy Point a network of creeks can be seen draining into Chichester Harbour. Many of the plants within the nature reserve still reflect this saline history. In the centre of the island are two sizable areas of woodland, Farm Copse and North Copse, while Tournerbury Wood is restricted to the ramparts of the fort. In the north-west, Stoke and Creek Commons exhibit extensive networks of salt marsh creeks. Much of this area was later converted into Oysterbeds. The importance of salt making on Hayling is amply illustrated by the numerous salterns along the eastern shoreline.

9

Water all around

Whimbrel and Ringed Plovers at Hayling Oysterbeds.

A detailed examination of the marine environment is beyond the scope of this book. However, one indication of the richness of these waters is that over 50 species of fish have been caught around Hayling Island. Many types of bird take advantage of this abundant source of food in the shallow, ice-free waters.

Red-breasted Mergansers

Diving duck, such as **Red-breasted Mergansers** and **Goldeneye,** make the harbours their winter home. Mergansers have long, serrated bills which they use to grasp fish in underwater pursuit. In contrast, Goldeneye have short powerful bills used for crushing shellfish and crustaceans. Both species breed in northern Europe, they use holes in trees for nesting. The newly-hatched chicks must jump to the ground and run to the nearest water where they are less vulnerable to predators.

Among the most adept at exploiting shoals of fish are members of the grebe family. The largest and most familiar is the **Great Crested Grebe** which, in summer, sports spectacular head plumes, once making it a target for the hat trade and driving it to the verge of extinction.
Now protected, numbers have increased greatly and it has become a common breeding bird on inland lakes and gravel pits. Great Crested Grebes, in their duller non-breeding plumage, spend the winter along the coast. Langstone Harbour holds one of the largest gatherings in Hampshire, often supporting over 100 birds.

Black-necked Grebe

Langstone Harbour is also one of the best places in Britain for observing the smaller **Black-necked Grebe**. A scarce breeding species in this country, the U.K. wintering population numbers around 100. In most years, a flock of up to 20 can be seen from the old Hayling Oyster Beds in the main Langstone Channel.

The similar looking **Slavonian Grebe** is also a regular visitor around Hayling. One or two are usually present off Black Point throughout the winter. Careful observation of the waters around the entrance to Chichester Harbour will sometimes reveal a **Red-throated** or a **Great Northern Diver**. Both species can be frustrating to see as they are capable of spending considerable time under the surface only to reappear some distance away.

Cormorant

Auks such as **Razorbills** and **Guillemots** spend the winter at sea far from their nesting colonies on sea-cliffs. Small numbers of both species may be encountered in the harbour entrances, usually in subdued winter plumage. The scarce **Little Auk** sometimes appears, often swimming close to the shore.

The distinctive silhouette of a **Cormorant,** with its wings outstretched, sitting on top of a channel marker, is a common sight all around the island. Unlike other waterbirds Cormorants feathers are designed to absorb water, which assists them when diving for food. After each dive Cormorants must dry their feathers to avoid becoming chilled, hence the familiar wing posture. Its smaller relative, the **Shag** is an uncommon visitor to the area. At home on rocky shores mainly in western Britain, individuals can occasionally be seen around the broken section of Mulberry Harbour in the south of Langstone Harbour.

Seabird passage

Many seabirds pass along the south coast of Hayling Island on their annual migrations. In May, 'seawatching' from Sandy Point can be rewarded with a passage of terns and skuas. Piratical **Arctic** and **Pomarine Skuas** pursue any tern they meet carrying fish, forcing the harassed bird to drop its catch. The skuas then acrobatically catch the falling food in mid-air. These migrants have spent the winter off the west coast of Africa and are returning north to breed in

Fulmar

12

Scotland and Scandinavia. May is also the best time of year to see continental species such as marsh-nesting **Black Terns** and **Little Gulls** which sometimes pass close to the shore.

Other birds involved in these annual movements include **Gannets, Fulmars,** divers and seaduck, such as **Common** and **Velvet Scoters.** A smaller return passage can sometimes be detected in the autumn but is far less pronounced than the spring migration.

Black-headed Gull

Summer Visitors

During the summer, the harbours around Hayling play host to a different cast of birds. **Little, Common** and **Sandwich Terns** return to breed on islands in Langstone Harbour. Sandwich Terns are among the earliest of returning migrants and their distinctive harsh call is one of the first signs of spring. These elegant birds gain protection by nesting amongst the large **Black-headed Gull** colony on the islands. The gulls aggressively attack any potential predators which approach the breeding sites too closely.

The islands in Langstone Harbour are owned by the Royal Society for the Protection of Birds (RSPB) and are wardened daily during the breeding season to ensure that there is no human disturbance .

The Little Tern is a nationally scarce species. In some years, such as 1988, the Langstone colony, at around 100 pairs, is the largest in the country. Recently a few pairs of Little Terns have successfully bred on a newly-created island in the Hayling Oysterbeds.

Little Terns tend to feed near the shore. They barely seem to get wet, as they deftly catch small fish in the shallow waters. Adult terns, with young to feed, can often be seen hovering over the harbour entrances or the deep-water channels at low tide.

Little Tern

13

The larger Common and Sandwich Terns prefer to fish further offshore and 'commute' back to the nest with their catch. By early autumn there are large numbers of adult and young terns in the harbours, their numbers boosted by migrants from further north. Many terns fly into Langstone Harbour at dusk, gathering in huge noisy groups as they prepare for the night. A good place to see this annual spectacle is at the Kench. Here, an offshore shingle bar makes an ideal safe roost site, sometimes for several thousand birds. By mid-October all but a few stragglers have left the island for their African wintering grounds.

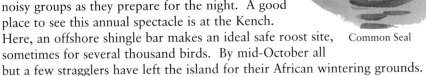

Common Seal

If you are lucky, you may catch sight of a **Common Seal** inquisitively poking its head above the surface of the water before diving again only to reappear many metres away. A small colony of these attractive mammals live in Chichester Harbour. Numbers are increasing and sightings around Hayling are becoming more frequent. The larger **Grey Seal** occurs mainly in western Britain and is a very rare visitor to the island.

Marine mammals are generally uncommon in the Solent. However **Harbour Porpoises** have been seen from the island, but only by very fortunate observers!

The Strandline

For beachcombers the strandline holds endless fascination. Both natural and man-made items from all over the world end their journey on the island's beaches. Following autumn gales the shoreline of south and west Hayling is strewn with many species of seaweed and other marine debris.

Kelp

Kelp is a large species of seaweed. Each kelp plant has a 'holdfast', a knobbly root-like structure, with which it is attached to a stone or rock. Having a rock anchor enables the plant to hold its position in the current. An indication of the power of some storms is seen when 2 metre kelp fronds, still attached to their erstwhile rock anchors, end up dumped along the high-tide line.

Red and brown seaweeds from deeper waters also litter the shore following severe weather. These seaweeds are often encrusted with *Bryozoa* or Sea-mats. Forming colonies on the surface of the seaweed, these simple animals feed by sieving the water.

Often washed ashore with this collection of seaweeds are **Oyster** shells, **Sea Squirts** and 'mermaid's purses', the black egg cases of **Dogfish** and **Rays**.

Every year, the mysterious white bones of **Common Cuttlefish**, so beloved of budgies, appear along the strandline. Cuttlefish are highly advanced members of the mollusc family, growing up to 30 cm long. They have five pairs of tentacles which they use for capturing prey.

Cuttlefish bones on the strandline.

Shoals of Cuttlefish enter the shallow waters around the island to spawn in mid-summer each year. Following this annual event, they die and their bodies are washed ashore, often in considerable numbers. If this happens during warm weather the smell can be unbearable and will linger on the beaches for weeks.

Mermaid's Purse

Making use of this abundant food source are armies of **Sandhoppers** and crabs which themselves are eaten by birds such as **Turnstone, Redshank** and **Rock Pipit**. The strandline has its own community of animals involved in recycling the detritus the tide leaves behind each day. Without them the shoreline would quickly be overwhelmed by the accumulation of debris.

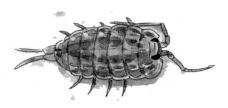
The Sea Slater is a large species of woodlouse. It inhabits the shoreline where it feeds on rotting vegetation.

Hayling Oysterbeds

The old oysterbeds at north Hayling lay abandoned until the 1980s when permission was given to rebuild the walls (or bunds) using imported building rubble. For several years this unnatural material was effectively dumped on an internationally important wildlife site.

Waders gathering to roost at The Kench.

Dennis Johnson

Oyster farming never restarted and by the mid 1990s the decision was taken by the owners, Havant Borough Council, to clean up the Hayling Oysterbeds. Much of the concrete rubble was removed creating a series of islands of varying heights.

The old oysterbed walls now accommodate a high-tide roost of tens of thousands of wading birds, one of the most spectacular wildlife sights on Hayling. The new islands are now used by breeding **Ringed Plovers, Oystercatchers** and Little Terns.

Several species of wader gather to roost at Hayling Oysterbeds. By far the commonest are Dunlin, which can number up to 20,000.

The Little Tern colony has grown rapidly and the Oysterbeds offer an opportunity to see these graceful birds at close quarters.

The creation of a salt water lagoon also provides sheltered feeding for Red-breasted Mergansers and Goldeneye. Over a period of time, it is hoped that the lagoon will develop the specialist community of marine invertebrates characteristic of this habitat. The whole area has recently been declared a Local Nature Reserve, and has a part-time warden, completing its transformation from dereliction to valuable wildlife site.

Dennis Johnson

Little Tern

Oysters

The **European Flat Oyster** *(Ostrea edulis)* occurs naturally in creeks and channels around the island. Oysters have probably been exploited by man since prehistoric times eventually leading to the development of a large fishery. Over-exploitation during the 19th century resulted in a decline in wild oyster numbers, and the introduction into Britain of oyster farming. The first British oyster beds were established on mudflats in Langstone Harbour during the 1860s. These oyster beds consisted of bund walls made from gravel and flint which prevented dredgers in the open harbour reaching the valuable oysters.

The oyster crop was shipped to London on the newly-opened Hayling Billy Line which passed close to the oysterbeds.

Oysters feed by filtering particles from the surrounding water, a technique which can result in pollutants being concentrated within the shell making them potentially highly toxic. The oyster industry on the island went into decline after 1902 when the Dean of Westminster was killed by food poisoning blamed on an oyster.

East Winner

The East Winner is a spit of sand extending nearly 3 km south from Gunner Point. Old maps indicate that the spit has extended over 300 metres since 1783 and it is still growing. At low tide, the East Winner is the haunt of thousands of gulls looking for food stranded on the surface by the falling tide. A few **Sanderling** and **Bar-tailed Godwit** also feed on the spit, but it is for its geological importance that the East Winner has been included in the Sinah Common SSSI.

Mudflats and Salt Marshes

The colourful marsh

Much of Hayling's most characteristic and important wildlife lies in the zone between land and sea, between high and low tide. Its unsuitability for agriculture means that it is perhaps the least modified habitat on the island, being largely unchanged for a thousand years.

From mudflat to salt marsh

Mudflats are formed when muddy water coming in on each tide is slowed by contact with the land, dropping its silt load to the seabed. Eventually this process reduces the waters depth enough for light to penetrate to the bottom and for plants to grow.

One of the earliest and most obvious pioneer plants is *Enteromorpha*, often called 'gut weed' due to its thread-like appearance resembling intestines. This prolific alga forms bright green carpets over the surface of the mud, easily visible at low tide. *Enteromorpha* stabilises the surface enabling the mudflat to grow further and faster. Eventually mud remains exposed above the water on some high tides and thus becomes a salt marsh.

Salt Marsh

Once mud is exposed for long periods of time, salt marsh plants can start to sprout. The first of these colonisers is **Glasswort** *(Salicornia)*, its scale-like leaves and round fleshy stems making it resistant to buffeting by tides. Perfectly adapted to its environment, this small plant traps further silt thus allowing other, deeper-rooted species such as **Cord Grass** *(Spartina)* and **Eel Grass** *(Zostera)* to gain a foothold.

As the salt marsh grows in height it is covered less often by high tide, enabling a wider range of plants to germinate. Salt marsh has 'zones' of vegetation caused by the varying frequency of flooding by salt water. In the middle zone, species such as **Sea Purslane, Thrift (Sea Pink), Sea Spurrey** and **Common Sea Lavender** all thrive in a diverse community alongside the specialist **Saltmarsh Grass** *(Pucinella)*.

In the upper salt marsh zone **Golden Samphire***, **Sea Wormwood** , **Saltmarsh** and **Sea Rush** can be found, usually growing with the salt-tolerant grass **Sea Couch**.

* *The name 'Samphire' applied to several unrelated coastal plants is derived from the French, 'Saint Pierre', a patron saint of fishermen, who reputedly walked on water.*

Eel Grass

The Eel Grass (*Zostera*) family is remarkable, being the only flowering plants in Britain which live entirely in salt water. More closely related to pondweeds than grasses, the inconspicuous flowers are even pollinated underwater. Once extremely common on the mudflats around Hayling, a disease in the 1930s all but wiped it out. A gradual recovery has seen Eel Grass return to large areas of Langstone Harbour where once again it is an important food source for Brent Geese and Wigeon.

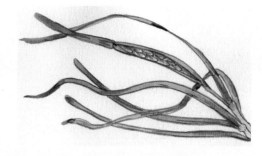

A network of creeks cuts across the salt marsh, draining both salt and fresh water. As these creeks become blocked by silt or vegetation, they form pans which retain water at low tide. During hot, dry weather these pans become very saline as water evaporates but after heavy rain the salt will become highly diluted. The pans often support their own communities of plants and animals able to survive in these extreme conditions.

During the spring, many of Hayling's salt marshes are bordered with the white flowers of **English Scurvygrass**. A member of the cabbage family, Scurvygrass contains large amounts of Vitamin C and was eaten by sailors on long ocean voyages to prevent scurvy. Its close relative, **Danish Scurvygrass** also occurs on the island. It has colonised roadside verges, responding to the gritting of roads in winter, the salt accumulates on the verges making them saline. This artificial 'salt marsh grassland' has enabled this plant to spread throughout the country. In spring, look out for its delicate pinkish flowers along the slipway onto the A3 at Broadmarsh.

English Scurvygrass

19

Salt marsh colour

A wet spring has some consolations as it can result in spectacular floral displays as here at Gutner Point. This carpet of Thrift or Sea-pink belies the image of salt marshes as dull colourless places.

This attractive perennial is found in almost every kind of coastal habitat. On Hayling it can be seen on sand dunes and shingle as well as in profusion on the salt marsh at Gutner Point.

During the autumn the Glasswort changes colour revealing an intricate pattern on the salt marsh.

Plants of the salt marsh

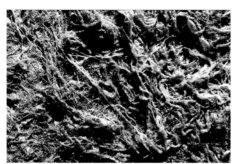

Enteromorpha - there are at least twelve species of this filamentous alga which live on mudflats. Growth begins in early spring and ceases in the autumn to leave extensive bleached mats at the edge of the marsh.

The bright yellow flowers of Golden Samphire are a familiar sight on the upper reaches of Hayling's salt marshes. The harbours around the Solent are the centre of distribution for this nationally scarce plant. The flowers can be seen from August to October.

Greater Sea-spurrey is a low growing perennial common on salt marshes all round the island. Its close relative Lesser Sea-spurrey has smaller, deeper pink flowers.

Sea Purslane - the silvery leaves of this shrubby salt marsh plant owe their colour to a covering of fine scales which help to reduce water loss. It often grows in broad swathes across the marsh.

Growing predominately in the middle of the salt marsh, Common Sea Lavender forms a vibrant blue carpet in mid-summer. When picked and dried it looses most of its colour. It is this species which is sold as so-called 'lucky white heather'.

21

The *Spartina* Story

Few grasses can survive emersion in salt water, but one which has adapted to saline conditions is **Cord Grass** *(Spartina)*. This is the plant whose distinctive yellow-green leaves form extensive beds across large areas of both Langstone and Chichester Harbours, sometimes extending for hundreds of metres from the shoreline.

The rise and fall of *Spartina* in the last 200 years has transformed the appearance of the harbours and has had serious consequences for erosion of the island's coastline.

For thousands of years there was only one species of *Spartina* in Britain, the native *Spartina maritima*, which was common on salt marshes. Some time early in the 19th century a species from North America, *Spartina alterniflora*, was accidentally introduced into Southampton Water, probably via shipping from the USA.

Spartina flowers

This introduced species combined with the native *Spartina maritima* to form the fertile hybrid *Spartina anglica*. Vigorous and able to grow much lower down the mudflats, *Spartina anglica* spread rapidly along the south coast forming vast beds, altering the appearance and wildlife of the harbours. It reached its peak in the 1940s when, in places, the original shoreline was raised by up to 2 metres. In contrast, the native *Spartina maritima* has declined drastically and may now be extinct on Hayling.

Old photographs of the 'Hayling Billy' often show the train travelling along the edge of Langstone Harbour with vast *Spartina* beds in the background.

Eroding *Spartina* saltmarsh, near Hayling bridge.

22

If you look at the same scene today only a few sorry remnants are left. Since the 1950s *Spartina* has been 'dying back'; the reason is poorly understood, but is possibly as a result of disease.

The protection from wave action these beds afforded, particularly along the west shore of the island, has been lost. The shoreline is now exposed to the full force of waves travelling across Langstone Harbour resulting in rapid erosion. It is remarkable how a single species of plant can have such an influence on the shape and appearance of the coastline.

Simon Colenutt

The Dunlin is the commonest wader in the harbours. Up to 30,000 spend the winter in Langstone Harbour.

Animals of the mudflats

Mudflats are amongst the most productive environments on earth. A constant supply of nutrients provided by twice-daily tides and the decay of animal and plant material lead to a few species occurring in enormous numbers. Birds have learnt a variety of feeding techniques to utilise this rich bounty.

In ideal conditions, the **Mud Snail *(Hydrobia)*** feeding on *Enteromorpha* and **Sea Lettuce** can reach densities of 50,000 per square metre. Each little larger than a grain of rice, these tiny snails play a vital role in the food chain of the harbours. Between tides they burrow into the mud before emerging to float, often considerable distances, on rafts of mucus. Washed up in their millions, Mud Snails form huge drifts along the strandline.

Mud Snails

Mud Snails are an important food source for a number of waterbirds including **Shelduck** which sieve the snails from the surface of the mud with a distinctive side-to-side movement of the head.

Black and white and the size of Brent Geese, Shelduck are easily seen on the mudflats around the island. A few pairs nest on Hayling, usually taking over old rabbit burrows. They are very secretive and difficult to find while nesting; the first sign is often a gang of ducklings dutifully following the parents around the marsh. In late summer most Shelduck migrate to moulting grounds in northern Germany. Shelduck from all over Europe gather there in vast numbers moulting most of their flight feathers, rendering them flightless until they regrow. By forming large flocks they have some degree of protection from predators while in this vulnerable state.

Cockles too, are prolific on parts of Hayling's shoreline. Like Mud Snails, they burrow just below the surface, moving up to feed when covered by the tide but they feed in a very different way. Instead of grazing on plant material they draw water into their shells via a long siphon, filtering off any food particles before ejecting the water through a second siphon. Occurring in densities of up to 500 per square metre, there are extensive Cockle beds off the western shore of Hayling Island. Several men still make a living by gathering Cockles as islanders have done for generations.

The main competition with these cockle gatherers is a bird, the **Oystercatcher**. Elegant in its black and white plumage with a bright orange bill, the Oystercatcher specialises in feeding on bivalve (two-shelled) molluscs. Despite their name Oystercatchers rarely feed on oysters, instead they mainly target cockles and mussels.

It has been shown that Oystercatchers use two techniques for opening shells: 'hammering' where the bill is used with brute force to break the shell, and 'stabbing' where the bill prises apart the two halves prior to extracting the Cockle. Each technique is handed down by the parent birds and will remain the same throughout the bird's life. Indeed the shape of an individual's bill will often indicate which technique it uses, with hammerers' bills being blunt-tipped and stabbers, pointed.

Over 2000 Oystercatchers regularly spend the winter in Langstone Harbour, a testimony to the richness of its cockle beds.

The Crustaceans are a major group of animals on the shoreline with the most familiar, the **Shore Crab**, the target of many a small boy with hook and line. Crabs will take live prey but are largely scavengers. The 'refuse collectors' of the shoreline they clean up any corpses washed up by the tide.

Shore Crab

Crabs moult their shells regularly as they grow and need to expand. These discarded shells or carapaces are often found along the strandline.

Corophium volutator

A less well-known but highly important member of the Crustacean family is *Corophium volutator*, an amphipod, 10 mm long, which makes shallow burrows in the mudflats' surface. Feeding on detritus, it can occur in prodigious numbers, up to 50,000 per square metre and is itself a vital food source for a number of wading birds.

The marine worms, **Lugworm** and **Ragworm,** are also major components of the harbour fauna. Preferring sandier conditions and growing to lengths of 200 mm or more, Lugworms live in U-shaped burrows. They feed by swallowing large quantities of sand which are sieved for food before being ejected to form characteristic 'casts' on the beach.

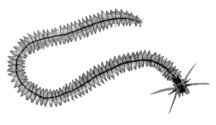

Ragworm

Ragworms are less fussy, occupying a wide range of marine habitats. They are free-moving, voracious predators with large jaws used for grasping their prey, mainly other small worms. Like so many mud-dwelling species they can occur in incredibly high numbers with up to 5,000 occupying a single square metre. Lugworms and Ragworms make up a large part of the diet of several species of wading bird.

Winter birds of the shore

Crucially for wading birds, the mild climate of the south coast coupled with salt water's resistance to freezing, ensures that the enormous food resource in the harbour's mud is available all winter. In addition, the relatively constant conditions within the mud enable its inhabitants to breed virtually all the year round, constantly restocking the larder.

Many species of bird which breed in more northerly countries spend the winter months around the mild shores of the British Isles. For students of ornithology, Hayling Island is ideally situated, with Langstone, Portsmouth and Chichester Harbours combining to form the most important site for wintering waterbirds on the south coast of Britain.

To many people, even to some birdwatchers, waders are just those 'brown jobs' out on the mud. "They all look alike" is a common complaint. It is perhaps unfortunate that we usually only see them in their drab winter plumage, designed to blend in with the muddy background.

Black-tailed Godwits in breeding plumage

Many wader species have startlingly bright breeding plumages. **Knot** and **Black-tailed Godwit** shed their dowdy winter colours and turn brick red, while **Grey Plovers** are transformed by a handsome black and white plumage. Even the humble **Dunlin** develops a jet black belly patch and reddish back feathers.

Most of these species leave the island in spring before acquiring this new plumage, but some return in August still resplendent in their full summer finery. Wader-watching in late summer gives a taste of the tundra breeding grounds where such seemingly gaudy plumage blends in with the russet colours of the local plants.

One wader which is usually remembered, even by non-birdwatchers, is the **Sanderling**. This dapper little bird, in its pale winter coat, is unmistakable as it runs rapidly along the shoreline like a wind-up toy. Sanderlings prefer sandy beaches to mud so their distribution in the harbours is restricted. Hayling holds the largest gathering of these birds in the county with the flock at Black Point sometimes exceeding 200.

Feeding

During the winter a wader's main preoccupation is finding food. The colder the weather the greater the amount of food required to maintain body temperature and the harder it becomes to find.

Waders have two main methods of finding prey, by sight and by touch. Species such as Grey Plover and **Lapwing** have large eyes (giving them excellent day and night vision) and short bills. They hunt by picking small items such as snails and crustaceans off the surface of the mud. **Golden Plover** have such good night vision that they often prefer to feed after dark, hunting for earthworms on grazing pastures. They roost out on mudflats during the day, usually in mixed flocks with Lapwings. A flock of several hundred Golden Plover spend the winter between Northney and Warblington on the mainland. Packed tightly together on a piece of salt marsh they stand out like a golden raft amid a brown sea.

Dennis Johnson

Dunlin, like many species of wader, probe the mud using their highly sensitive bill-tip to detect any food items. Many of the small invertebrates Dunlin feed

Curlew

26

on become more active and move closer to the surface as the tide begins to cover them. To exploit this, Dunlin follow the moving tide line. You can often see them strung out like a line of beads feeding at the water's edge.

Larger species such as **Curlew** and Black-tailed Godwit also use this technique, but with longer legs and bills are also able to feed in shallow water. The Curlew is the largest European wader. Equipped with a long bill designed to reach

Turnstone

lugworms deep in the harbour mud it will turn readily to earthworms in arable fields following wet weather.

Redshanks employ both methods, feeding by sight during the day, when *Corophium* are their main target, and switching to mud snails at night which they locate by touch.

A third technique is employed by the appropriately named Turnstone, which uses its short powerful bill to turn over stones and seaweed while searching for food. Turnstones are thinly spread along the island's shoreline and, being well camouflaged, are often hard to spot. The only time they gather together in any numbers is at high tide roost sites.

Dennis Johnson

Roosting Dunlins, Turnstones and Grey Plover

Roosting

Waders are unable to feed during the high tide period so many gather at traditional roost sites. With many eyes keeping a look out, roosting in large numbers offers a degree of protection from predatory birds such as **Peregrine Falcons**. Huddling close together in harsh weather conditions also helps the birds retain heat. Hayling has several high tide roosts which often hold spectacular numbers of birds. On some tides over 20,000 Dunlin gather at Hayling Oysterbeds. When disturbed, they take flight in vast wheeling flocks which change from dark to light as the birds move in unison, almost like drifts of smoke. This behaviour is an important defence mechanism, confusing predators by making it extremely difficult for them to pick out an individual target amongst the moving mass.

Other important roost sites on Hayling Island are at Black Point, The Kench, and Gutner Point.

It is vital that waders at roost sites are left undisturbed, especially in cold weather when they need to retain energy to keep warm.

Just passing through

Some waders breeding in the northern Britain, Iceland and the Arctic spend the winter, not in Britain, but in Africa. This group of species pass through the harbours around Hayling on spring and autumn migration.

Whimbrel, smaller relatives of the Curlew, move through in April and again in September when their far-carrying seven whistle call is a familiar sound over the island. In autumn, up to 100 can gather to roost with Curlew at Gutner Point.

Several other species, including **Common Sandpiper, Greenshank** and **Spotted Redshank** also pass through in spring. These birds are in a hurry to reach their breeding grounds and seldom stop for more than an hour or so. **Curlew Sandpiper** and **Little Stint** are more common as autumn visitors, often mixing with other waders at roosts such as the Hayling Oysterbeds and The Kench.

Breeding Waders

Few of the thousands of birds which winter around Hayling stay to breed. Most migrate north for a brief summer on the vast wilderness of the Arctic tundra. Those which remain must find an area of suitably undisturbed habitat on this busy holiday island.

Dennis Johnson

Redshank on nest.

28

Lapwings were once a common breeding bird on Hayling Island. Numbers have greatly declined, as they have over most of lowland Britain, due to the advent of intensive arable farming. Where Lapwings could once raise a family in arable fields, the crops are now sown in the autumn and are too high in the spring, their eggs being shaded out before they can hatch. The use of pesticides has also reduced the amount of food available to any chicks which do survive. Despite these changes, a few pairs still hang on. The Lapwing's acrobatic territorial display flight can still be seen over several grazing marshes on the east coast of the island each spring.

Redshanks usually make their nests in the long grass at the upper reaches of a salt marsh. The nest must be high enough to avoid being flooded on spring tides, but remain hidden from predators such as **Foxes**. Loss of this rough grassland habitat mean Redshanks no longer breed on the island every year, but a pair still occasionally brings off a brood in a quiet corner. Year-round residents of the harbours, Redshanks, unlike other waders, are notoriously site faithful and are loathe to move during cold weather. During the hard winter of 1962/63 their population was decimated but has since recovered.

Wildfowl also make use of the abundant source of winter food on mudflats and salt marshes. **Brent Geese**, Shelduck and several species of 'dabbling duck' are common around the islands saltings.

No bigger than a Woodpigeon, **Teal** are the smallest of Europe's ducks. At home in salt marsh creeks, they use their specially adapted bills to sieve fine particles from the water surface or they up-end to reach vegetation on the muddy bottom. When disturbed, small groups explode into rapid low flight before diving down again into the next creek.

A loud, slightly plaintive whistle is often the first indication of the arrival of a flock of **Wigeon**. These attractive ducks are long-distance migrants, returning each winter from their breeding grounds in northern Russia. Strictly vegetarian, they graze on Eel grass in the harbours and will sometimes come ashore like Brent Geese to feed on sown grasslands.

Both these species of duck are still legal quarry, but today wildfowlers take few around the island.

Wigeon

Kingfishers are normally associated with inland rivers, where they excavate breeding holes in the bankside. Cold weather will sometimes cause fresh water streams to ice over thereby preventing the birds from catching fish.

Kingfishers

To overcome this potential hazard many Kingfishers migrate to the coast for the winter. These colourful birds are a regular feature at Hayling Oysterbeds and around Northney where they often sit motionless for hours waiting for a catch.

Another patient fisherman is the **Grey Heron** which patrols the creeks and channels of the saltings all around the island.

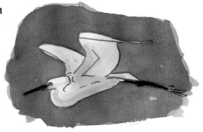

Today, Grey Herons are outnumbered locally by **Little Egrets** which have shown a remarkable increase in the last 20 years. Populations of birds change over time, often for reasons we do not fully understand.

Little Egret

Little Egrets were once hunted for their spectacular white plumes which were used in the making of ladies' hats. Driven to extinction in northern Europe during the 19th century, their protection was one of the reasons behind the formation of the Royal Society for the Protection of Birds (RSPB).

Legal protection allowed a gradual process of recolonisation through France, the first Hampshire record occurring in Langstone Harbour in 1957. Little Egrets remained rare visitors to Hampshire until 1989 when an unprecedented late summer influx was followed by several birds overwintering on Hayling Island.

Since then the annual arrival has grown each year, with up to 300 roosting on Thorney Island and in Tournerbury Wood during the year 2000. This gathering of Little Egrets is the largest in the UK, with birds now a daily sight from Langstone Bridge.

The colonisation of this country by these elegant birds was completed, when in 1996 several pairs nested on Brownsea Island in Poole Harbour. It may only be a matter of time before they also nest on Hayling Island.

Grey Herons build large nests in the tops of trees. Herons at the nest are very wary and will fly off at the slightest sign of an intruder.

How do we know how many birds there are?

Huge numbers of waders and wildfowl use the harbours around Hayling Island, but how do we know how many there are?

The answer to this question is provided by a remarkable series of monthly counts.

The Wetland Bird Survey (WeBS) is a joint scheme of the British Trust for Ornithology (BTO), The Wildfowl and Wetlands Trust (WWT), Royal Society for the Protection of Birds (RSPB) and the Joint Nature Conservation Committee(JNCC) to monitor non-breeding waterbirds in the UK.

WeBS counts take place each month on all major wetland sites in Britain, including Langstone and Chichester Harbours. A dedicated team of volunteers located at strategic points around the harbours record all waders and wildfowl in their section. The mass of information collected enables the totals for each species in each location to be calculated. The information is published in an annual report which includes totals for the country as a whole.

Langstone Harbour has the longest continuous set of these monthly counts from anywhere in the Europe. Starting in 1952, and continuing to this day, they provide an invaluable record of the changes in fortune of many of our most important bird species.

During the winter, Langstone and Chichester Harbours support about 20 birds per hectare of mud, the highest density of any estuarine site in the UK.

The good news is that long-term trends for the majority of species covered by the WeBS counts show an increase in numbers. This situation has been brought about by a reduction in shooting pressure, including the removal of many species from the list of legal quarry, and the protection of many important wintering sites such as Langstone Harbour.

Wader counting at Hayling Oysterbeds.

Black-headed Gulls are so common that they rarely get a second glance but, in recent years, another species, the slightly larger, **Mediterranean Gull** has started to appear with them on Hayling. In breeding plumage they are striking birds with heavy blood-red bills, jet black heads and white wing-tips.

Originating from the Black Sea area, Mediterranean Gulls have moved steadily westwards, breeding for the first time in the UK at Needs Oar Point, Hampshire, in 1968. The expected colonisation was slow with only 11 pairs in Britain by 1990.

Black-headed Gull (above) and Mediterranean Gull. Note the white wing-tips, bright red bill and black hood of the Mediterranean Gull.

In the last ten years, Mediterranean Gull numbers have significantly increased with over 80 pairs nesting in the United Kingdom by the year 2000. Locally, in Langstone Harbour, 38 pairs nested amongst the large Black-headed Gull colony making it the most important breeding site for the species in the country.

Mediterranean Gulls can be seen around Hayling at any time of year, but spring and summer are best. Look out for them in flocks of Black-headed Gulls, especially in the entrance to Langstone Harbour.

Insects on the edge

A salt marsh may seem a harsh environment for insects and spiders. A few species have adapted to living in this habitat, their eggs, able to survive long periods of immersion in salt water, may even be carried to new areas by the tides.

The leaves and flowers of Sea Aster provide food for the **Star-wort moth,** the caterpillars occur in two colour forms, purple and green, each beautifully matching the

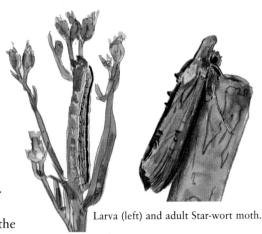

Larva (left) and adult Star-wort moth.

stems of the foodplant. The adult moth is camouflaged as a piece of broken twig and is rarely seen.

The **Sea lavender Plume** moth *(Agdistis bennetii)* is perfectly camouflaged amongst the dead stems of salt marsh grasses. As its name suggests, its larva feeds on sea lavender.

Sea Lavender Plume moth

The **Lesser Marsh Grasshopper** can be abundant amongst the grasses growing on sea walls at the Kench and Oysterbeds. It is usually a plain brown colour with a pale stripe along its wings but also has green and pink forms which are well camouflaged amongst the leaves of **Sea Beet**.

Lesser Marsh Grasshopper

The striking **Wasp Spider** *(Argiope bruennichi)* can be found in the same areas as the grasshopper. Wasp Spiders are recent arrivals in England, the first being seen at Rye Harbour, East Sussex, in 1922. They colonised the Hampshire coast during the 1970s. The large females eat the tiny males shortly after mating. They then mature during late summer and autumn when they can easily be found on their webs waiting for prey. The web has a distinctive white zig-zag pattern in the middle, the only British spider to have this feature. This may serve to reflect warmth on to the spider's body or help to make the web more easily visible to large flying insects and birds, which could destroy the web. The females spin papery egg cocoons during the autumn. These can be seen during the winter months attached to grass stems.

Wasp Spider with egg cocoon.

Wasp Spider - showing the distinctive zig-zag pattern in its web.

33

BRENT GEESE

The Fall and Rise of Brent Geese

Large flocks of Brent Geese are a familiar sight around Hayling during the winter months. The story behind these charismatic birds' remarkable migrations and their changing fortunes at the hands of man make them one of our most interesting visitors.

Of the four forms of Brent Goose in the world, three regularly visit the harbours around Hayling: the North American and Asian race or 'Black Brant' is a rare visitor to this country; the Pale-bellied race breeds in Arctic Canada, Greenland, Svalbard and Franz Josef Land and winters in Jutland, north-east England and Ireland, a few can be seen around Hayling most winters; and the Dark-bellied race which winters mainly in south-east England, Holland and France. It is this last race which is such a characteristic sight around the island.

Black Brant   Pale-bellied Brent Goose   Dark-bellied Brent Goose

The entire population of Dark-bellied Brent Geese breed around the remote Taimyr peninsula in northern Siberia. The journeys they make to and from these breeding grounds are remarkable.

As day-length and temperature increase during March, the Brent leave the harbours around Hayling and head east at the beginning of their migration. During April and May they gather in huge numbers in Holland, Denmark and Germany around the Wadden Sea. From here they depart in late May, flying directly to the White Sea where they rest for a few days before completing the 3000 mile journey to the Taimyr Peninsula in the middle of June.

Breeding pairs nest on the Arctic tundra where they begin a race against time in which they must lay eggs, incubate them and fledge their goslings before the Arctic winter sets in once again. Their diet consists mainly of the mosses and lichens which carpet the barren tundra. After the breeding season, the adult birds moult their wing feathers making them temporarily flightless. By the end of August, the Brent have left the Taymyr; any birds still unable to fly will die as the weather gets colder and their food disappears under ice and snow.

Young Brent Geese

The geese follow a similar route on their return journey, the first birds arriving back in the UK around mid-September with the majority returning during October and November.

A close look at the newly-arrived flocks will reveal the success of the year's breeding season. The young birds of the year have neat white edges to their wing feathers making them

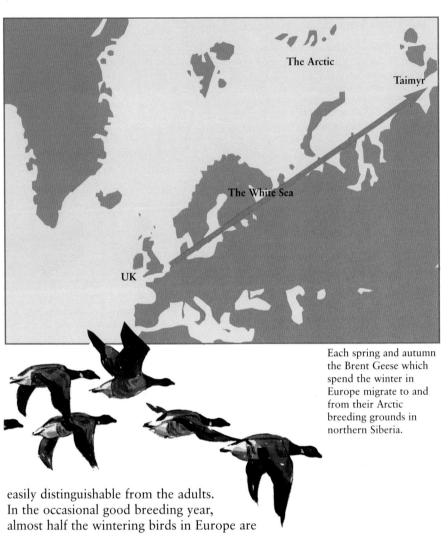

Each spring and autumn
the Brent Geese which
spend the winter in
Europe migrate to and
from their Arctic
breeding grounds in
northern Siberia.

easily distinguishable from the adults.
In the occasional good breeding year,
almost half the wintering birds in Europe are
juveniles. Breeding success is closely linked to the Lemming population on
the tundra. In good 'lemming years' predators have an ample food supply
and do not bother the Brent Geese. Most years however, breeding success is
low due to predation by Arctic Foxes, Herring Gulls and Snowy Owls which
will take most, if not all, of the chicks.

Brent Geese mate for life and families remain together through a young
bird's first winter. If you watch a flock carefully it is possible to see that it is
not a random collection of birds but distinct groups of families and pairs
without young.

Brent Geese numbers have fluctuated enormously during the last 100 years, largely due to the activities of man. At the beginning of the 20th century the world population of Dark-bellied Brent was around 50,000. By the 1930s an increase in hunting pressure and improvements in guns had started a serious decline in their numbers.

Brent Geese

Dennis Johnson

By 1955, the world population was estimated at only 16,500 birds and there were real concerns for their long-term survival. A series of conservation measures in Britain and other European countries, including a ban on hunting and protection of important wintering sites, such as Langstone Harbour, has resulted in a remarkable recovery. Today, the world population stands at over 250,000 with 40 per cent wintering in the UK. Locally, numbers have increased from a mere 700 in the 1950s to nearly 20,000 birds which overwinter in the area today.

One factor which has undoubtedly helped this recovery is a change in diet which took place in the early 1970s. These shy birds, which formerly fed exclusively on salt marsh plants out on the harbour mudflats, started to feed on playing fields and cereal crops adjoining the harbours. This has led to some conflict with farmers as the geese trample winter wheat and eat large amounts of sown grass leys. This resilience and adaptability bodes well for the future of the species as Brent have learnt to exploit the man-made habitats which today surround the harbours. Long may they thrive.

Brent Geese

Sand dunes and Shingle

Sea-holly

'Far more than just a beach'

The southern coastal strip of Hayling Island consists of a mixture of sand and shingle deposits upon which some of the finest maritime plant communities in Hampshire have developed.

Unfortunately many visitors to the island see only the long and apparently barren shingle beach around Hayling Bay. Mobile shingle, such as this, forms up to a quarter of the British coastline. Shingle is a very hostile environment in which to survive. Plants and animals must avoid being crushed by the movement of stones during winter storms.

Shingle is surprisingly good at retaining fresh water as it clings to the surface of individual stones. Try putting your hand into a shingle beach on a hot day and see how cool and damp it feels. In droughts, plants growing in shingle often survive longer than those in normal soils.

Tides bring in seaweed and animal corpses which decay along the strand line providing nutrients. Shell debris is ground up filling the gaps between the stones and preparing the shoreline for its first plant colonists. Not until the movement of shingle has been stabilised can pioneer species finally gain a foothold.

Gunner Point

Gunner Point lies at the south-west tip of the island and is a relatively recent feature having developed over the last 150 years due to movements of shingle along the shoreline. The Point is still growing and has left behind it a series of ridges, each progressively more stable and with greater plant cover. Gunner Point is probably the most important vegetated shingle beach in Hampshire. In June, thousands of **Sea Kale** plants bedecked in white blossom provide a wonderful natural spectacle. A hardy, long-lived perennial, its deep roots are somehow

Sea Kale at Gunner Point

able to extract the nutrients it needs from the beach. Being a member of the cabbage family, the young leaves make excellent eating and were widely gathered in the past. Other plants living on the beach such as **Sea Beet** and **Sea Radish** were also exploited for food. Gunner Point supports the largest Hampshire population of the nationally scarce plant **Little-robin**. In summer, many thousands of this diminutive member of the Geranium family can be found here scattered amongst the ridges.

Behind the current storm beach is an area of exceptionally rich grassland which has developed on the old fossilized beaches. In April and May, several thousand **Green-winged Orchids** grow here amongst the parasitic **Yellow Rattle** whose yellow flowers give way to brown seed pods which rattle in the wind. Another parasitic species, **Eyebright,** also occurs here, its roots tapping into those of surrounding plants. It was used in the past to treat a wide variety of eye complaints. In mid-summer, a multitude of clovers and **Wild Thyme** are punctuated by the tall blue flower spikes of **Viper's-bugloss** and occasionally the rare **Nottingham Catchfly.**

With such a wealth of wild flowers it is unsurprising that Gunner Point attracts numerous butterflies. In favourable years literally thousands of **Common Blue** butterflies dance across the ridges searching for mates or their foodplant, **Bird's-foot-trefoil.** Vivid orange **Small Copper** butterflies and more subdued coloured **Small Heaths** are abundant. Huge numbers of **Six-spot Burnet** moths busily crowd the flowerheads of Viper's-bugloss.

Green-winged Orchid

Birds too make a living here. From early spring, the cascading song of **Skylarks** carries across the point. **Meadow Pipits** breed in the long grass, scurrying rapidly away as you approach. In spring and autumn migrant **Wheatears** and **Whinchats** spend a few hours refuelling on the beach before moving on. In winter, flocks of **Greenfinches** and **Linnets** hunt for seeds among the ridges.

One bird which truly makes the beach its home is the **Ringed Plover.** Every year a few pairs attempt to nest, laying up to four perfectly camouflaged

Skylark

40

eggs in a shallow scrape. The black-and-white sitting adults are remarkably difficult to see against the stony background. If an intruder approaches too close to the nest the plover will lure them away with an elaborate 'broken wing' display, fluttering weakly ahead as if injured. When it feels secure it suddenly flies off, returning to the nest only when the coast is clear. In the past, birds such as Ringed Plovers would have nested freely on Hayling's shingle beaches alongside other species such as Little and Common Terns. Today increased levels of disturbance have led to a serious decline in the breeding success of this attractive wader.

If you find a Ringed Plover's nest (or any bird's nest) please leave it well alone.

Ringed Plover eggs (top) and adult on nest.

Dennis Johnson

'Hayling's Sandhills'

'The shore which gently slopes to meet the ocean, extends several miles and is covered with the finest and most beautiful of sands'

Topographical and Historical Account of Hayling Island (1826)

Hayling has long been famous for its 'sandhills'. In old postcards of the island, they can often be seen as a backdrop to happy holiday scenes. Once extending from near the ferry terminal round to the site of the 'Inn on the Beach', they provided a wonderful playground for people and a hugely important area for wildlife. Today, although much reduced in size, Hayling still boasts the only sand dune systems in Hampshire.

In addition to the dunes at Sinah, there are those at the Sandy Point Nature Reserve in the south-east corner of the island and some recently developed dunes around the sailing club at Black Point. It is probably only at this last site that sand dune formation is still occurring naturally on Hayling. Dunes develop on gently sloping sandy shores. Whenever an onshore wind blows faster than 10mph, sand is driven inland and when it falls below this speed the sand is deposited. Debris scattered along the strandline traps the moving sand causing it to accumulate. Rotting vegetation provides enough nutrients for early colonising plants to become established. On Hayling, three species are frequently encountered on this part of the beach. **Sea Rocket** has seed pods dispersed by high tides, **Prickly Saltwort** has fleshy leaves, each tipped with a sharp spine, the bane of many a sunbather, and **Frosted Orache** whose leaves have a glistening, frosted appearance. Although able to survive in this mobile landscape, these species do little to stabilise the shifting sand, a job that falls to the grasses.

Moss Carder Bee *(Bombus muscorum)*. This local species still occurs at Gunner Point.

Sand Couch and **Lyme-grass** have roots which penetrate the loose sand binding it together and enabling the main dune forming species, **Marram,** to become established.

Marram grass has an amazing root system able to extend up to nine metres (30ft) per year. In favourable conditions, dune growth can be very rapid enabling other species to exploit the gaps between the marram tussocks. On the dunes at Sinah, **Sand Sedge** is easily distinguished by the rows of regular green leaf spikes marching across the surface. More colourful residents include **Yellow Horned-poppy, Sea-holly** and **Sea Bindweed** which thrive on the bare sand areas.

Many of these coastal plants have very restricted distributions in Hampshire. **Sea Spurge** is common on Hayling Island, but is found in only two other locations in the county. Its yellowish-green flowers are a magnet to the many species of bees and wasps which make their nest burrows in the warm sand. Hayling has long been famous amongst entomologists for the variety of rare insects which inhabit its sandhills. Several species new to the British Isles were first recorded on the island; testimony to its mild climate and ideal habitats.

Sandhills at Gunner Point with Marram grass in the foreground.

The **Robberfly** *Philonicus albiceps* is often encountered on Hayling's dunes, one of the few places it can be seen in Hampshire.

A large number of moth species, many rare or local in Hampshire, occur on Hayling's sandhills. The **Grass Eggar**, a smaller version of the familiar day-flying Oak Eggar, is common on Gunner Point in August. This area is also the county's stronghold for **Sand Dart**, a dune specialist whose caterpillars feed on Prickly Saltwort. In recent years the

Robberflies grasp their prey with their powerful legs often taking large insects like this Small Heath butterfly.

rare and attractive pyralid moths *Cynaeda dentalis* and *Sitochroa palealis* have been found on the island. Both may be recent colonists, perhaps indicating a long term change in climate.

Dune Slacks

Developing in the low-lying depressions behind dunes or between two dune ridges, water-retaining 'dune slacks' often contain a rich flora. Dune slacks are particularly well developed on the large dune systems of western Britain with its high annual rainfall.

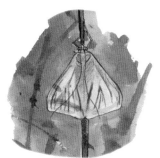

On Hayling, the sand dunes are too small for the development of extensive slacks but at Sandy Point, a plant characteristic of this habitat survives in a small area behind the main dune. **Sharp Rush** is the largest member of its family in Britain and as its

The Carrot moth
Sitochroa palealis

name suggests has incredibly sharp pointed stems. The small colony at Sandy Point is the only site between Devon and Kent where this impressive plant grows.

Creeping Willow is found in both dune slacks and heathland. Common in the New Forest but with an outpost on Hayling Island, Creeping Willow still grows on the Hampshire Wildlife Trust Reserve adjacent to the golf course.

A description in *The King Holds Hayling* (1961) reads *'the marsh hollows are golden with the fluffy catkins of the miniature willow'* which indicates that Creeping Willow has probably declined in abundance on the island in recent years.

Hayling's sandhills face a number of threats, some natural and some man-made.

Sharp Rush at Sandy Point.

To remain in a healthy and dynamic state, dunes require a constant supply of fresh sand. At both Gunner Point and Sandy Point, this supply appears to be interrupted as the beaches immediately in front of the dune systems are now largely shingle. Without new sand, the dunes gradually become 'over mature' with Marram grass and bramble forcing out the more specialist plants like Sea-holly which need open sand on which to grow. Eventually this natural succession will lead to the dunes being completely covered with scrub, losing much of their wildlife value. At Sandy Point Nature Reserve, the County Council, by clearing scrub and creating open areas, is attempting to reverse this process.

Brown Argus- small colonies of this butterfly survive on the dunes at Sinah Common and Sandy Point.

Only at Black Point, where a combination of a continuing supply of fresh sand and some fencing by the Sailing Club, are new dunes being formed.

A second, and perhaps more serious threat to the survival of Hayling's sandhills, is the sheer pressure of recreational use. Trampling and fires have reached such a level at Gunner Point that the naturally resilient dunes are unable to repair themselves and are eroding rapidly. Unless some measures are taken to control this level of pressure, one of Hayling's and Hampshire's most important wildlife sites could well be lost forever.

Not all is doom and gloom however, while much of the sand and shingle habitat has been damaged or destroyed by development over the last 200 years, a great deal still remains. To the west, the opening of Sinah Golf Course in 1884 protected an important area from almost certain development in the 20th century. In recent years too, Havant Borough Council has taken an enlightened view in managing its Beachlands estate by preventing indiscriminate parking and cutting much of the grasslands more sympathetically. In 1999, the importance of the area was finally recognised by English Nature, the government body responsible for nature conservation, when it was declared a Site of Special Scientific Importance (SSSI). Hopefully this will help protect a uniquely important area for future generations of islanders and visitors to enjoy.

Photo courtesy of Havant Borough Council

Gunner Point - from the air. The damage caused to the dunes by trampling is visible as a large patch of open sand.

Flowers of the dunes

Sea Bindweed is a close relative of the notorious garden 'weed' but unlike that species is very much restricted to the coast.

Sea-holly looks similar to a thistle, but actually belongs to the Cow Parsley family. Many butterflies and other insects are attracted to its flowers in late summer.

Hare's-foot Clover, named after its fluffy seed head which resembles a hare's foot, is widely distributed along Beachlands preferring areas of recently disturbed sand.

Sea Sandwort is a succulent low-growing perennial with insignificant white flowers. This tough little plant is able to survive in mobile shingle and will re-sprout even when completely buried.

Yellow-horned-poppy is named after its long seed pods which, when touched, split open, violently scattering seeds. Its delicate flowers seldom last more than a day as the petals are blown off by even the gentlest breeze. The attractive glaucous green leaves are covered with fine hairs to prevent water loss in this arid environment.

45

Life amongst
the rocks

Hayling Island has no natural
rocky shores such as those
commonly encountered in south-
west England. In such locations, a
community of specialist animals
and plants develops, able to
withstand the pounding of waves
and the constant change brought
about by the tides.

The installation of large-scale rock
revetments as a sea defence
around part of the Eastoke
peninsular has enabled the gradual
colonisation by species normally
associated with rocky shores and
not found elsewhere on the island.
The rocks, each weighing around
three tons were imported by lorry
from Somerset in 1990.

Rock groyne

Carefully placed to form a series of groynes projecting into the sea, they have
developed an interesting series of zones depending on their level of exposure
to wave action. Those nearest the sea have become smothered with
Barnacles and large numbers of **Limpets**, the limpets themselves often
encased with barnacles. Deeply embedded in the
rock fissures are small groups
of **Mussels** and with them
the shiny, glutinous blobs of
Beadlet Anemones, their
tentacles withdrawn at
low tide. No large algae
seem able to survive here.
Only microscopic plants
upon which the limpets feed
can grow.

Further up the groyne is a
band of rocks covered with a

Purple Sandpiper

variety of seaweeds. Most of these species of 'wrack' have gaseous bladders which allow the weed to float freely and maximise the amount of sunlight they are exposed to while in the water. At the top of the groyne away from the splash zone the colourful rocks are devoid of life.

A bird which specialises in feeding on rocky shores can occasionally be seen jumping fearlessly from boulder to boulder just feet from the breaking waves. The **Purple Sandpiper** is well-camouflaged in this environment, its mustard yellow legs the only concession to bright colour. It feeds on small crustaceans living in cracks and amongst the seaweed fronds.

Beadlet Anemones

Great care should be taken when exploring rock groynes. Always be aware of the state of the tide and use sensible footwear. You should always have somebody with you.

Limpets and Barnacles encrust the rocks.

Heathland

Grayling

Our Heathland Heritage

There are fewer more colourful sights than a heath in high summer - drifts of purple heathers punctuated with dazzling yellow gorse, alive with the drone of bees.

Heathland is a man-made habitat developing on poor acidic soils like those of the New Forest and parts of the Hampshire coast. Three thousand years ago Bronze Age man cut down the remaining 'wildwood' to create pasture for his domestic stock. Over time, as nutrients were washed from the soil, it was heathland, not rich pasture, which developed, characterised by a community of dwarf shrubs dominated by heather.

For several thousand years, vast tracts of southern England, including much of Dorset, north-east Hampshire and Surrey were covered with lowland heath. Unable to support large numbers of livestock, heathland was farmed traditionally by low intensity grazing. Being of little economic value, lowland heath became a victim of agricultural improvement, housing development and large scale forestry. In the 20th century over 80 per cent of lowland heath was destroyed in southern England.

The southern coastal strip of Hayling Island consists of infertile gravels and sand which have readily turned to heath. Being unable to support arable

Maritime heathland at Sandy Point - a nationally scarce habitat.

49

crops, this area was largely open Common Land until the middle of the 19th century. Hundreds of years of grazing by commoners' livestock and wild rabbits created an intricate mosaic of heathland and grassland. At one time, this habitat would have extended from Hayling Island across Southsea Common and over to Browndown, near Gosport, where a substantial remnant of heathland now lies within a nature reserve.

On Hayling today, these once extensive 'waste lands' have been eaten away by the demands of housing and recreation but, in a few places, the heather still blooms each year as a reminder of past glories.

Common Heather or Ling

Heathers
Heathland derives its name from heather. Heathers are dwarf shrubs, the definitive heathland plants. Three species of heather grow naturally in Hampshire and all still occur on Hayling Island.

Common Heather or **Ling** is the most widespread in the UK. It is this species which covers vast tracts of the uplands and which makes up most of the New Forest heaths. Its pale mauve flowers appear in August just as summer starts to fade. On Hayling, the only remaining extensive patches of Ling are at Sandy Point.

Rarely found growing together because of their subtly different habitat requirements are the two species of *Erica* heathers. **Bell Heather** (*Erica cinerea*) has glossy green leaves, deep pink flowers and prefers light well-drained soils. By contrast, its relative, **Cross-leaved Heath,** (*Erica tetralix*) has grey-green leaves and

An unusual photograph of Hampshire's three heather species growing side by side at Sandy Point Nature Reserve.

Several substantial strips of Bell Heather remain on Sinah Golf
Course forming, in summer, spectacularly colourful 'rough'.

pale pink flowers. Mainly a plant of damp boggy conditions, Cross-leaved
Heath is most at home on wet heaths. Bell Heather grows extensively
alongside the fairways on Sinah Golf Course, and provides an attractive verge
to Ferry Road opposite the Kench.

At Sandy Point, the windblown coastal heath on the seafront has developed a
unique community of Bell Heather, lichens and stonecrops on the parched
gravelly soil. The lichen heath here is the most extensive in Hampshire.

The rarest of the trio on Hayling is Cross-leaved Heath which is restricted to
a few small clumps at Sandy Point. Its clusters of rose-pink flowers often last
late in to the season, occasionally until November.

Heathers produce an enormous amount of seed which can remain viable for
up to 100 years. Clearing trees from areas of former heathland will often
result in the germination of long-dormant heather seed lying in the soil. At
Sandy Point, efforts to re-establish heather on areas which had become
covered with scrub are proving successful. With the assistance of grazing by
the introduction of Highland Cattle it is hoped in time to recreate at least
part of Hayling's heathland heritage.

Gorse

At both Sandy Point and Sinah Common, extensive banks of Gorse form impenetrable thickets, burnished golden yellow in spring with coconut-scented flowers. During hot weather in late summer, patches of gorse maintain a constant crackling sound as ripe seed pods explode.

There are three species of gorse native to the UK, Sandy Point on Hayling Island is one of the few places where all three grow together. The commonest, **European Gorse**, is notoriously easy to burn and was familiar to our ancestors who used it for lighting fires.

Gorse- the dominant shrub of the heathland landscape, gorse can be found in flower somewhere on the island in every month of the year, hence the old country saying 'when furze(gorse) is in bloom, kissing's in season'.

The diminutive **Dwarf Gorse** can be found growing amongst the heather at Sandy Point and Sinah Common. Flowering in late summer, its small spines afford little protection from browsing rabbits which often clip the bushes into rounded 'pin cushions'.

The third, **Western Gorse**, is a species found mainly in the south-west and Wales. In 1980, the eminent botanist Dr Francis Rose discovered Western Gorse growing at Sandy Point, a surprising find and the first record for Hampshire. Like Dwarf Gorse, Western Gorse flowers late in the summer but has longer curved spines and is a more robust plant.

Western Gorse appears almost delicate alongside its larger relatives. Usually a plant of south-west England it grows on the Sandy Point Nature Reserve.

Common Dodder is a parasitic plant of Heather and Gorse. Its long, filamentous stems have given it the colloquial name of 'Devil's Guts'. Dodder is not rooted in the ground and its scale-like leaves have no chlorophyll. Instead, its stems are modified roots which penetrate the host's tissue to extract nutrients. Bearing white flowers in mid-summer this must be one of Hayling's most curious looking plants.

Plants of the heath

English Stonecrop occasionally spreads prolifically through the turf creating a mosaic pattern of white and green.

Trailing like a mass of spaghetti over gorse and heather at Sandy Point, the parasitic Common Dodder is a curious sight. The long tendrils are modified roots which enter the host plant's tissue to extract nutrients.

Sheep's Sorrel - this slender member of the dock family thrives on acid soils. It appears like a red carpet made from hundreds of individual flower spikes.

The delicate blue flowers of Sheep's-bit look out of place amongst the woody stems of heather. It can be seen in flower at both Sandy Point and Sinah Common.

Pale Heath Violet - this beautiful member of the violet family is rare in Hampshire except in the New Forest. The purple-veined petals and long slender leaves make this an unusually distinctive violet. Pale Heath Violet flowers in most years at Sandy Point.

Birds of the Heath

Compared to ancient woodland, heathland is home to relatively few species of bird. Those which do occur have adapted to use heathland plants for feeding, nesting and shelter.

Linnets are small seed-eating finches once common on farmland throughout the country. Intensification of agriculture has caused a dramatic downturn in their fortunes and today heathland provides one of their last strongholds. Linnets nest in loose colonies often in banks of Gorse. In spring, breeding males, with bright pink breasts and crimson crowns, sit on high perches to sing their rambling musical song. Linnets can often be seen on Sinah Golf Course and in the nature reserve at Sandy Point.

The harsh, scolding call of a Dartford Warbler emanating from deep within a Gorse clump is one of the most evocative sounds of spring on Hayling. Always active, Dartford Warblers will seldom perch for more than a second or two before whirring rapidly to the next bush, trailing their long tails behind them. The easiest time to see these usually skulking birds is when they have young to feed. At this time they move around in noisy family parties.

For a bird more at home on the hillsides of the Mediterranean, it seems remarkable that the **Dartford Warbler** not only survives on Hayling but stays here throughout the winter. Dartford Warblers are true heathland specialists. In Britain they are virtually confined to southern lowland heaths, nesting in thick Gorse scrub and hunting for insects amongst the Heather.

In the hard winter of 1962/63, the Dartford Warbler population in Britain was decimated. By the end of that terrible winter it was estimated that there were fewer than ten pairs left in the country, all in the New Forest.
Fortunately, Dartford Warblers breed rapidly and a series of mild winters has led to the population recovering and old sites, including those on Hayling Island have been re-colonised. The first record of Dartford Warbler on Hayling comes from 1894 when it was said to have bred. Today, several pairs nest at both Sandy Point and around the golf course at Sinah. This healthy situation is reflected nationally with numbers of pairs currently amongst the highest ever recorded. It seems that the Dartford Warbler may be one species which will benefit from the effects of climate change.

The **Stonechat** derives its name from its curious call which sounds like someone hitting two stones together.
A classic bird of the heaths, Stonechats have the habit of sitting on a prominent perch, calling loudly and flicking their wings as you approach.

Stonechat

Invariably found as a pair, male and female Stonechats look very different. Males are colourful with bright orange chests, jet black heads and, when flying, startlingly white shoulder patches. As with most species of bird, the female has a duller, mainly brown plumage, but with good reason as she is the one who incubates the eggs. In most years, Stonechats breed in gorse scrub at Sandy Point and Sinah Common. In autumn, Hayling often receives an influx of migrant Stonechats which spend a week or so on the island before moving on.

While Stonechats are year-round residents, **Whinchats** are summer visitors. Frequenting similar heathland haunts to Stonechats, Whinchats appear on Hayling only on migration. Easily told by their broad pale eye-stripes and white tail markings, Whinchats are seen in small numbers every year. The maritime heath at Sandy Point is particularly attractive to another migrant bird, the **Wheatear**. Newly-arrived male Wheatears make a fine sight as they sit atop gorse bushes on early April mornings. Always one of the earliest migrants to return in the spring, male Wheatears arrive back from Africa before the females. Passing rapidly through Hayling on their way north to establish territories amongst upland moors and mountainsides, Wheatears vanish as quickly as they arrive.

During their return migration, small flocks of Wheatears often gather on the golf course searching for insects in the short turf of the fairways before heading out across The Channel.

When Wheatears fly they reveal a bright white rump which gave them their old country name of 'white arse'. This was far too vulgar for some Victorian naturalists so the name was altered to 'Wheatear'.

Reptile Heaven

Reptiles love heathlands. Being cold-blooded, they require warmth from the sun in order to become active. The many open sandy areas found on heathlands are ideal for basking and egg-laying. Heathlands support populations of all six of our native species of reptile. On Hayling Island, four of these species are found, but none are confined to heathland.

The reptile with the largest population on Hayling is the **Slow Worm**. This legless lizard occurs in huge numbers at Sandy Point. Experiments here using sheets of metal to attract Slow Worms have found some of the highest densities ever recorded in Britain (up to 2000 per hectare). So common are Slow Worms at Sandy Point that in spring it is not unusual to find a dozen or more sheltering under a single metal sheet.

Slow Worms can be found in most open habitats on Hayling. Once reviled because of their resemblance to snakes, today Slow Worms are often encouraged into gardens as they feed largely on pest such as slugs.

Slow Worms do not lay eggs, but give birth to live young. About 75 mm long and a golden-sandy colour, young Slow Worms look very different from the grey-brown adults. Long-lived animals, Slow Worms can survive up to 15 years in the wild, while one kept in captivity lived to be 54!

Common or Viviparous Lizards love to bask on wooden fences, walls and other man-made structures. On cold spring mornings they can be found soaking up what little heat the weak sunlight affords. Once warmed-up, Common Lizards are fast, agile movers and good climbers. On cool days, they often need to 'recharge their batteries' and will return regularly to a favourite basking spot.

Like Slow Worms, Common Lizards give birth to live young which are born, seven or eight at a time in mid-summer. The small, all-black young lizards can sometimes be seen sunbathing on paths but, like their parents, once warmed up they can vanish in an instant.

There are no authentic records of the larger **Sand Lizard** on Hayling Island. A rare species found only on lowland heath and coastal sand dunes, Hayling may well have supported a population in the past. Degradation of suitable habitat on the island means that if they were once present, they have now been lost.

Adders require open sunny glades with thick cover nearby and are at home on heathlands, in woodland rides and on railway embankments. They seem to like the rough of golf courses in particular.

Adders hibernate from October to March usually in old rabbit burrows. After emerging in spring, Adders will often bask for several weeks in a favoured spot prior to shedding their skins and going in search of a mate. Adders feed mainly on small

The Common Lizard is one of the most northerly-distributed reptiles in the world. Tolerant of cold Common Lizards will sometimes emerge from hibernation during February and have even been observed basking between patches of snow.

mammals but will also take lizards. The live young are born in late August or September just a few weeks before they must go into winter hibernation. Despite their venomous reputation, fewer than 100 people are bitten by Adders in Britain each year and there have been no fatalities for over 20 years.

Strangely, there are no Adders in the Sandy Point Nature Reserve despite it being ideal habitat. It seems they were eradicated by the previous owners, worried that patients might try to pick them up. Isolated from other populations on the island, it appears that there is no way for the Adder to naturally recolonise the reserve.

Simon Colemutt

North Hayling Church Wardens' Accounts reveal that people were paid 2d per head for killing Adders. In 1816, 227 adders were killed for this bounty alone. The practice of paying people to kill snakes ceased in 1836, but Adders were still widely persecuted well into the 20th century.

Adders are shy creatures which prefer to avoid contact with man. *If you find an Adder please do not harm it or attempt to pick it up.*

Grass Snakes are usually found near water. They swim readily and prey on frogs and toads. They are uncommon on Hayling with few recent sightings.

Insects of Heathland

Heathland has only existed in its current form for 3,000 years, not long enough for the development of a diverse insect community. Despite this, a number of species are heathland specialists, often occurring in huge numbers.

Grayling butterflies are numerous at Sandy Point and on the Hampshire Wildlife Trust reserve at Sinah Common. Mottled brown and white undersides provide superb camouflaged for these butterflies which spend most of their time resting on the ground. Their caterpillars feed on grasses in the spring and only at night.

Another butterfly, the **Brown Argus,** occurs in low numbers at Sandy Point and Sinah Common, the only coastal sites in Hampshire. It is actually a close relative of the Common Blue and, like that species, spends much of its time sunning itself on low vegetation. Its caterpillars feed on Common Storksbill.

The **Bordered Grey** moth is a local species in southern England, usually found in the New Forest. The ancient coastal heaths of Hayling hold a small colony of Bordered Grey moths. Usually nocturnal, they can occasionally be disturbed from the heather during the day.

Grey Bush-cricket

The high-pitched calls of the male **Grey Bush-cricket** are a familiar sound amongst the heather in summer. This species is exclusively coastal in this country, Hayling and Eastney supporting the only Hampshire colonies. Sandy Point and Sinah Common have particularly large colonies of Grey Bush-crickets.

A rising buzz is usually the first indication of the presence of the **Mottled Grasshopper**, a small species which inhabits areas of very short, rabbit-grazed turf. It has distinctive clubbed antennae and is amongst the first of the grasshoppers to mature and begin singing, usually in early June.

The **Lesser Cockroach** inhabits patches of heather where it feeds on decaying vegetation. This native species is not a pest but, like its notorious cousins, is a very fast runner. A small colony exists at Sandy Point where it is occasionally found under stones and heather during the late summer.

Lesser Cockroaches

Sandy Point

The largest and most important remaining fragment of heathland on the island is now protected within the Sandy Point Nature Reserve. Formerly part of Eastoke Common, the 17.4 hectares of Sandy Point were enclosed to form the grounds of the Lord Mayor Treloar Hospital in 1919. Whilst most of the surrounding land was built on during the 20th century, Sandy Point has remained untouched, like a time capsule preserving the island's wildlife.

Gradually the importance of the plants and animals which survive at Sandy Point has been realised and the area has been given some protection. When Chichester Harbour was declared a Site of Special Scientific Interest (SSSI) the grounds to the hospital were included. By the mid-1980s, the Local Health Authority who owned the site had no further use for it and part of the land was sold to the County Council. In 1988, Sandy Point was designated a Local Nature Reserve.

The value of Sandy Point lies in the remarkable range of habitats protected within a relatively small area. Sand dunes skirt the southern and eastern boundaries while a mosaic of maritime heath and acid grassland has developed on the coastal shingle. The centre of the reserve comprises a mixture of saline grassland, a relic of an old salt marsh creek and gorse scrub. The northern area consists mainly of scrub with a network of grass footpaths originally laid out within the hospital grounds. The extraordinary variety of wildlife recorded at Sandy Point makes it a unique site in Hampshire, and its survival even more fortuitous.

Photo courtesy of Hampshire County Council

Aerial view of Sandy Point.

Ancient Grasslands

In Britain, grasslands like heathlands are largely man-made environments. Grassy clearings in the wildwood were enlarged and kept free of scrub regrowth by cutting and burning. Fire encouraged new grass growth, providing more food for animals. By grazing domesticated livestock, man has modified the landscape, creating a range of different grassland habitats each adapted to the local climate and geology.

In Hampshire, the beauty of the vast open chalk downs was created by thousands of years of sheep-grazing producing a grassland turf incredibly rich in wildflowers. On neutral and acid soils, grazing resulted in a different assemblage of species dependent on that particular environment.

A close look at one of these 'ancient grasslands' will reveal that they contain relatively little grass. Ancient grasslands have an abundance of flowering plants all competing against each other for space and nutrients, but with none dominant over the rest. The plants which survive must be able to tolerate grazing or regular cutting for hay.

Meadows
On Hayling as elsewhere, there are two main types of meadow.

Hay meadows, usually on the better ground, were kept for growing a hay crop which was cut and dried in high summer. Sheep were then allowed to graze the regrowth.

Grazing meadows (or pastures) were often on the poorer soils. Here animals were grazed all year round, being fed hay during the winter. The plant communities which developed in these two types of meadow were often very different.

West Lane fields

Ancient Grasslands

Modern, more intensive farming techniques have resulted in the loss of most ancient grasslands. Since 1949, over 95 per cent of old meadows have been destroyed making them amongst the most threatened habitats in the UK.

Grasslands were either ploughed up for arable crops or reseeded with a single grass species such as **Rye Grass**. Where old meadows have survived they are often given large doses of fertilizer to improve the yield. Increased levels of nutrients lead to a reduction in the number of grassland plants because one or two species become dominant and out-compete the rest. The change from hay to silage, which is cut much earlier in the year, also has a detrimental effect on grassland insects such as butterflies which are unable to complete their life cycles before the silage is cut.

Many of today's grasslands have virtually no wildlife interest and are little more than 'green deserts'. Ancient grasslands, which were once commonplace in the countryside, have now become so rare that many of those which survive are protected as nature reserves.

On Hayling, much of the fertile and well-drained land was used for growing arable crops. Meadows were largely restricted to land adjacent to the harbours. Even a quick glance at a modern map of the island reveals that this pattern is still maintained. Many of the grassland fields which skirt the island are now regarded as important wildlife sites and have been given legal protection.

Indicator Plants

Certain species of plant can only survive in one type of habitat. For example, some species will only grow in the shade of a wood while others are found solely in damp meadows or on chalk downland. These plants are known as 'indicator species' because they are indicators of a particular type of habitat.

Usually, the more 'indicator species' found in a particular location, the richer that habitat. For example, Sandy Point has 41 acid grassland indicator species, the highest total for any single location in the UK.

Dyer's Greenweed - a classic indicator species of ancient grasslands.

Grazing animals
For hundreds of years, sheep grazed the fields and commons of Hayling. Cattle were a rarity on the island because beef was expensive, a luxury food for the rich until the 20th century. Recent upheavals in farming have meant that there are now very few grazing animals on Hayling.

A small herd of **Highland Cattle** graze the Sandy Point nature reserve during the summer, while the island's last surviving dairy herd can still be seen at Northney. The two most important grazing animals on Hayling today are the rabbit and the horse.

Prior to the last few decades, the only horses on Hayling were working animals used for drawing carts and ploughing. The

Highland cattle are ideal for grazing the nature reserve at Sandy Point as they will readily eat coarse vegetation and even trees! The cattle are used to control the spread of scrub and to manage the flower-rich grassland.

huge increase in the popularity of recreational horse-riding has resulted in a large number of horse paddocks appearing all over the island. Horses graze using the teeth at the front of their mouths and thus crop the turf short. These horse-grazed paddocks develop a characteristic flora.

In certain areas, rabbits and even Brent Geese are important grazing animals, often coming into conflict with the farmer.

West Lane Fields
These are a series of interconnecting meadows adjacent to the Hayling Billy Line. The 'West Lane Fields' contain some of the most flower-rich grassland on the island.

In spring, brown patches of **Divided Sedge** stand out against the prevailing green sward. Green-winged Orchids appear in

Grazing by horses favours certain species. Horse paddocks in spring often have drifts of yellow buttercups as horses do not eat them.

most years, but these fields really come into their own in high summer. July sees swathes of yellow **Dyer's Greenweed** bisect the fields from end to end. One of the few plants to give a reliable yellow colour, it has been used to dye wool for over 1000 years. Combined with indigo, it produces a vibrant green. The leaves of Dyer's Greenweed are often peppered with the curious homes of the case-bearing moth *Coleophora vibicella*. This rare species is found in abundance in this one part of the island.

A fine display of Dyer's Greenweed in the West Lane fields. Examination of its flowers reveals its close affinity to Gorse.

Dotted amongst the long grasses are the rotund white flowerheads of the extravagantly named **Corky-fruited Water-dropwort**. A

The case-bearing moth, *Coleophora vibicella* and larval case on Dyer's Greenweed.

plant of ancient unimproved grassland in southern England, it has declined along with many other meadow species. Less demanding in its requirements is **Common Knapweed**, a familiar plant of roadsides and meadows all over Hampshire. Highly attractive to bees and butterflies, knapweed flowers throughout the summer months and spreads readily if not cut.

Insects of the meadow

Walking through a summer meadow to the gentle accompaniment of a chorus of grasshoppers is one of the highlights of the year. The appropriately named **Meadow Grasshopper** is the key player in this chorus and is found in grassy areas all over the island.

Moving rapidly from flower to flower, **Meadow Brown** butterflies are still common

Meadow Grasshopper

63

Burnet moth larva and cocoon (above).

The male Six-spot Burnet moths take to the wing first and mate with the females as they are emerging from their cocoons.

where the grass is not cut too early. **Small Heath,** another member of the 'brown' family has declined on many parts of Hayling but can still be seen around the West Lane fields throughout the summer. Both **Small Skipper** and the very similar **Essex Skipper** enjoy the abundant nectar from knapweeds and thistles.

The day-flying red and black burnet moths are sometimes so common they seem to fight for space on a favoured flower-head. There are two similar species, the **Narrow-bordered Five-spot** and **Six-spot Burnets,** identified by the number of red spots on each forewing.

Far more abundant than these 'showy' species are the myriad of spiders and leaf hoppers which make their homes out of sight among the grass stems. One species however leaves you in little doubt as to its presence.

The **Yellow Meadow Ant** makes impressive mounds from individually sorted grains of soil. When the grass is long the mounds can be difficult to see, but when heavily grazed by rabbits they stand out like islands in a green sea. These anthills grow slowly, the largest ones (up to a metre across) are thought to be over 100 years old. As these anthills are easily destroyed by mechanical cutting or ploughing, their presence indicates that the field has not been cultivated for a long time. The short coastal grassland at Gutner Point contains a number of large anthills attesting to its long history of grazing.

Each anthill is a sophisticated home for the colony. Constructed from fine particles, the anthills are free-draining so avoid becoming waterlogged in wet weather. The temperature within the mound varies by only a few degrees throughout the year creating ideal conditions in which the ants can reproduce.

Ant hills at Gutner Point.

The Yellow Meadow Ant is the favourite food of the **Green Woodpecker**. Unlike the other British woodpeckers, Green Woodpeckers feed mainly on the ground using their powerful bills to break into anthills and their long sticky tongues to extract the ants. The laughing call of the Green Woodpecker can be heard wherever anthills abound.

Along the harbour shore
Clinging to the shoreline of north-east Hayling are a series of rough grazing meadows extending south from Northney Farm to Gutner Point. These fields, traditionally grazed by sheep, have often been at the mercy of the tides and 300 sheep were drowned when seawater flooded in from the south in 1917. Today, only a few cattle graze here but the meadows retain many plants associated with saline coastal grassland.

Ants are a favourite food of the Green Woodpecker.

In low-lying brackish areas Sea Rush and Saltmarsh Rush provide a rough bite for the cattle. The saline influence can be seen in the sprawling presence of Greater Sea-spurrey and **Sea Milkwort** and in the patches of Divided Sedge. These ditches also provide the only Hayling locality for the scarce **Brookweed**.

On the drier ground grow Dyer's Greenweed and **Spiny Rest-harrow,** both apparently untouched by the attentions of grazing cattle.
This series of meadows are of high wildlife and landscape value and for this reason are protected within the Chichester Harbour SSSI.

Many of the old sheep-grazed meadows around Gutner Point and along Woodgaston Lane have been turned over to horse paddocks. In a few of these fields orchids still flower and in one particular garden there is a spectacular annual display of Green-winged Orchids. Often found growing with Green-winged Orchids is the strange fern **Adder's-tongue** which likes the same old unimproved grasslands.

Land from the sea

Hayling has seen little significant land reclamation when compared with neighbouring Portsea Island. One area where man has intervened is Tournerbury and Middle Marshes on the island's eastern shore. Middle Marsh was originally embanked in the 17th century, the land gradually being converted from salt marsh to sheep pasture. When Tournerbury Marsh was also enclosed a large area of rough grazing land had been created which remains to this day.

The soil of this reclaimed land was always too saline for growing crops. Consequently it has never been ploughed. The abundance of large anthills is testament to the long history of grazing on the marsh, as are the meadow indicator plants, **Distant Sedge** and **Meadow Barley.**

From the air, the original layout of salt marsh creeks can still be seen on the reclaimed land.

Adder's-tongue is a mysterious fern appearing one year only to vanish the next. It gets its name from the projection, said to resemble an adder's tongue, emerging from the centre of its single leaf. It was once used as a remedy for snake bite.

These depressions retain water and are colonised by both the tall spikes of **Sea Club-rush** and the slender submerged **Beaked Tasselweed**.

As with the fields in the north-east of the island, a characteristic flora has developed at Tournerbury with salt marsh species and meadow species combining to form a distinctive coastal grassland.

These reclaimed marshes are one of the last places on Hayling where you can see **Grey Partridge**. Once very common all over the island and widely shot for sport, changes in farming methods mean it is now restricted to a few unimproved grasslands.

In a survey of meadows carried out by the County Council in the 1980s, Hayling Island was found to have some of the best remaining coastal meadows in Hampshire. Due to their diverse plant life, Tournerbury and Middle Marshes have been included in the Chichester Harbour SSSI.

Commons

One hundred and fifty years ago Hayling had a series of commons. The commons were areas of rough grazing land where local people could turn out their animals. These lands were usually fairly infertile and therefore supported a wide range of animals and plants unable to compete in the cultivated landscape.

Gradually, by Acts of Parliament these commons were enclosed and the use of the land changed forever. Within a short period of time at North Hayling, Creek Common (1868), North Common (1870), Stoke Common (1874) and Verner Common (1876) were enclosed. When South Common was finally enclosed in 1886 the era of common lands on Hayling, and the wildlife they protected, had come to an end.

North Common

Against the odds, a slice of historic Hayling has survived at North Common, Northney. Much of the original common has been improved for agriculture or been tipped on, but an area of rabbit-grazed grassland and scrub retains many species characteristic of unimproved coastal grassland.

A sea of Bird's-foot-trefoil at North Common. The country name for this plant is 'eggs and bacon' referring to its yellow flowers and orange buds.

In spring, the ground glows yellow with a carpet of Bird's-foot-trefoil which attracts numerous Common Blue butterflies. In wet hollows behind the sea wall are pockets of Sea Milkwort, Divided Sedge, Saltmarsh Rush and the scarce **Slender Hare's-ear**, an extremely small member of the Cow Parsley family. Plants uncommon elsewhere on the island such as **Pepper Saxifrage, Hairy Sedge** and **Common Spotted Orchid** also grow here. The careful observer might spot the extraordinary **Strawberry Clover**. Its flowers resemble other clovers, but the seed heads which appear in late summer look just like strawberries. August sees drifts of **Common Fleabane** spread across

Common Blue butterflies lay their eggs on the young leaves of Birds-foot-trefoil. Female Common Blues are generally brown with a row of orange dots at the edge of the wing.

the turf. Its yellow flowers seem irresistible to butterflies making North Common one of the best places on the island to see migrant **Clouded Yellow** and **Painted Lady** butterflies.

Attracted by the abundance of grasshoppers, Wasp Spiders set their silken traps amongst the tall grasses, often startling early blackberry pickers. North Common is a good place to see migrant birds with **Redstarts** and **Spotted Flycatchers** being annual visitors. The occasional rarity such as the **Wryneck** is always a possibility in autumn.

North Common is a small jewel of a site which deserves to be well-protected. Now in the ownership of Havant Borough Council, the common has been declared a SINC (Site of Interest for Nature Conservation).

Creek Common and Stoke Common
The arrival of the railway on Hayling in the 1860s was the final nail in the coffin for Creek and Stoke Commons. A large chalk bund was built to provide a solid base for the line as it crossed marshy ground. The bund bisected the two commons, effectively cutting their eastern sides off from the sea. The marshy western half of Creek Common, formerly the haunt of breeding Redshanks, was used for tipping on in the 1960s. The remaining

field retains its original network of creeks and dykes which still harbour some of the plants associated with salt marshes. Today the line of these creeks is picked out by a luxuriant growth of rushes and dotted with the lilac flowers of **Sea Aster**. On raised ground, both **Common Centaury**, and its scarcer relative, **Lesser Centaury**, grow in profusion.

Brackish ditches are the domain of Sea Aster. Resembling a squat Michaelmas Daisy, these colourful plants flower throughout late summer.

In the early years of the 20th century, Stoke Common boasted a population of the rare **Saltmarsh Goosefoot**. Sadly, this plant has long gone and is now extinct in Hampshire. Much of Stoke Common has reverted to scrub and woodland following the abandonment of grazing by commoners.

Chalk-loving plants from the adjacent railway bank have spread into the coastal turf where **Yellow-wort**, a downland plant, is an unusual find.

The rough grass of Creek Common supports large populations of small mammals, especially **Field Voles,** making it a popular hunting area for **Kestrels**. This is also one of the best places on the island to see **Barn Owls**.

South Common

Following its enclosure, most of South Common came into public ownership and it now forms Beachlands. To the east of the golf course is an area of fixed sand and shingle, part of which is used as a car park.

This area is remarkable for its number of small flowering plants including an incredible variety of

In some years, such as 1947, 1983 and 2000, migrant Clouded Yellows appear on Hayling in considerable numbers. Those which arrive in the spring often breed on the island, their caterpillars feeding on clovers and Bird's-foot-trefoil.

69

clovers. A close look is required
to really appreciate them, but in
June a few minutes on your hands
and knees should reveal **Suffocated
Clover, Rough Clover, Knotted
Clover, Subterranean Clover** and
Fenugreek as well as other small
annuals such as **Shepherd's Cress**
and the rare **Mossy Stonecrop**.
This part of Beachlands is a
botanist's paradise, with a large
number of rare and local grass
species including **Bulbous
Meadow-grass,** recorded here for
the first time in Hampshire in
1932.

The historical management of
South Common has left Hayling
blessed with one of the richest
vegetated beaches in Hampshire.

Rabbits

Flower rich grassland on South
Common near The Crescent.

Rabbits were being farmed in
Britain as early as the 13th century.
Vast warrens were stocked with thousands of rabbits which were an important
source of meat. Dry sandy soils were favoured for rabbit farming so the south-
west of Hayling was ideal.

The name, Sinah Warren, was first recorded in 1443 and lives on today in the
name of a holiday village. Old maps reveal the extent of the warren which
covered an area larger than today's golf course.

Away from the warrens, rabbits remained relatively scarce
in the countryside until the 19th century. The increased
popularity of hunting led to the extermination of
predators such as foxes by gamekeepers and free from
natural predation the rabbit population exploded. Rabbits
became a major agricultural pest.

In 1953, the deliberate introduction of a disease,
Myxomatosis, resulted in rabbits dying in vast numbers.
Spread by the **Rabbit Flea,** myxomatosis killed 99 per cent
of rabbits contracting the disease. Today, many rabbits
have developed an immunity, but every few years
myxomatosis returns to the island and the sight of blind
and docile rabbits becomes commonplace again.

Rabbit

Following the abandonment of commoners' grazing on Beachlands, rabbits maintain many of the important grassland habitats. Their constant nibbling preventing the development of scrub.

Sandy Point

Sandy Point Nature Reserve contains a mosaic of different types of grassland. In spring, the short turf behind the sand dunes comes alive with tiny points of colour as **Spring Vetch, Early Forget-me-not** and **Wall Speedwell** emerge from their dormant seeds. Early summer sees a profusion of clovers flowering on the dry paths often with the strange flower spikes of **Common Broomrape** pushing up between them. As the season progresses, **Lady's Bedstraw,** lemon yellow **Mouse-ear Hawkweed** and towering Viper's Bugloss take over. Growing on the back of the dunes is **Hound's-tongue,** a plant said to smell of mice!

The remnant of a salt marsh creek, formerly connected to Chichester Harbour, forms the centre of the reserve. The soil here retains a high level of salt which is reflected in the unusual plant community it supports. **Parsley Water-dropwort,** Saltmarsh Rush and the rare **Long-bracted Sedge** all grow here while on drier ground, a large colony of **Dotted Sedge** occurs at its most easterly location in the British Isles.

During harsh winter weather this low-lying wet ground sometimes becomes home to **Snipe** and **Woodcock** escaping the frozen conditions further inland.

Acid grassland often develops alongside heathland on acidic sandy soils. Hayling Island and Sandy Point Nature Reserve in particular, have some of the most species-rich acid grassland in Britain.

Growing on the network of paths within the reserve are a number of plants characteristic of acid sandy soils. **Tormentil, Lousewort, Heath** and **Common Milkwort** appear in profusion in the short rabbit-grazed turf. Where water lies in winter, the tiny annuals **Allseed** and **Blinks** occur at one of their few Hampshire sites outside the New Forest. Enclosed within Sandy Point are sizeable areas of neutral grassland. Here the white umbrella-like flowerheads of **Wild Carrot** dodge the attentions of grazing Highland Cattle. **Grass Vetchling** is almost impossible to see in the long grass, until the appearance of its exquisite slender-stemmed crimson flowers.

Intriguingly, several plants more commonly associated with chalky soils, are also found

Snipe

growing at Sandy Point. **Pyramidal Orchid, Autumn Lady's-tresses** and **Carline Thistle** appear from time to time, growing alongside acid-loving plants. The explanation for this appears to lie in the large amount of ground-up shell debris found in the sandy soil. The shells of marine animals are made from calcium carbonate (chalk) and it is this which enables these species to survive here.

With so many potential food and nectar sources available, it is no surprise that Sandy Point Nature Reserve supports an enormous range of insects. The colourful **Cream-spot Tiger** and the **Cinnabar** moths both occur here. The distinctive black and yellow-striped caterpillars of the Cinnabar feed on **Common Ragwort** often stripping the plants of all their foliage.

The varied soil conditions at Sandy Point have resulted in a remarkable array of grassland types, helping to make it one of the most important wildlife sites on the Hampshire coast.

Sea Walls

Many of Hayling's sea defences are of fairly ancient origin. Some sea walls were mown or grazed, but most were spared applications of fertilizer and over time, they have developed a distinctive and rich flora. Even recently built sea walls such as those around Northney Marina, constructed during the 1970s, support healthy populations of **Narrow-leaved Bird's-foot-trefoil** and Grass Vetchling. Upper salt marsh plants like Sea Wormwood and Golden Samphire will readily colonise the lower reaches of sea walls, while the scarce Slender Hare's-ear prefers the tops of the banks. **Fennel** and large stands of **Teasel** characterise some sections, the latter attracting winter flocks of **Goldfinches** in search of seeds.

The dense growth of Sea Couch on the sea walls around Northney appears to be ideal habitat for the **Essex Skipper** butterfly. This species, which is very similar to the Small Skipper only arrived on Hayling in 1990 following a prolonged period of range expansion. The Essex Skippers seem to be more tolerant of salt spray than Small Skippers. This may explain why Northney is one of the few places in Hampshire where they far out-number their usually commoner relatives.

The numerous rabbit burrows in some defences are a favourite breeding site for Shelduck. The adults brood their young safely out of sight well underground. Hayling's sea defences are an excellent example of the way wildlife can utilise almost any available habitat.

The spectacular Cream-spot Tiger moth can sometimes be disturbed from long grass at Sandy Point.

72

Grassland flowers

Lady's Bedstraw has a pleasant fragrance when dried and was formerly used for stuffing mattresses. It was also said to discourage fleas.

Lousewort is a short-stemmed perennial which is partly parasitic on other nearby plants. At Sandy Point it grows commonly on the paths, attracting pollinating bees.

The broomrapes are parasitic plants gaining their nutrients from the roots of their host species. Common Broomrape parasitises a number of species of clover.

The white flowers of Autumn Lady's-tresses spiral around the flowerhead. At Sandy Point numbers of this species fluctuate greatly from year to year.

A tall biennial found commonly on stable sand dunes, Hound's-tongue acquires its name from its deep red flowers, which are supposedly the colour of a hound's tongue.

Fresh water

Hayling is a low lying island in an area of little rainfall, consequently it has few natural areas of fresh water. The only flowing water on the island is the 'Cranbrook', a small brook meandering across private land at Tournerbury. Herons from the nearby heronry in Tournerbury woods have no doubt fished the brook for centuries giving it the alternative name 'Heron Stream'.

For many years the only sizeable water bodies on Hayling were farm ponds and ponds on common land. A pond formerly in the south-west corner of North Common is still in existence today, but now lies adjacent to a sharp bend on Northney Road.

Latterly the growth in the number of garden ponds has helped in supporting the island's aquatic wildlife.

Sinah Gravel Pit
During the early 1940s the Hayling Golf Club allowed the excavation

Sinah Gravel Pit

of a substantial quantity of gravel from land adjacent to the course at Sinah. The excavation soon filled with water and Sinah Gravel Pit was formed. By far the largest area of fresh water on the island, the gravel pit has developed an interesting variety of wildlife.

During winter months Sinah Gravel Pit regularly plays host to flocks of over one hundred **Tufted Duck** and similar numbers of **Pochard**. These diving ducks are sometimes joined by their scarcer relative the **Scaup** which tends to appear following harsh weather. Another species which occasionally takes refuge during hard weather is the **Bittern**. This now very rare member of the Heron family has appeared on several occasions with three present around the gravel pit throughout the 1981/82 winter. Elusive **Water Rails** are also annual winter visitors.

Coot are resident on the gravel pit with up to a hundred birds present in winter and a dozen or more pairs breeding. In most years a few pairs of Tufted Duck attempt to breed along with **Little Grebes**, which build their nests on platforms of floating vegetation.

Water Rail

74

During their spring and autumn migrations, both Little Gulls and Black Terns often spend an hour or two hawking over the gravel pit. These essentially marsh birds may be attracted to any large areas of fresh water on their travels.

Little Grebes feed on insects and small fish which they catch by swimming amongst underwater vegetation. They nest on a floating platform made from water weed and will sometimes raise two broods in a year.

Groups of Gulls, including the occasional Mediterranean Gull, enjoy bathing in the freshwater of Sinah Gravel Pit. **Long-eared Owls** sometimes roost in the thick scrub around the pit which is one of the best places on the island for birdwatching.

In the north-east corner of the gravel pit is a small enclosed pool. This area has developed a rich wetland flora with both **Fringed** and **White Water-lily** and a small bed of **Common Reed** which attracts **Reed Warblers** and **Reed Buntings**. The shingle banks here are covered with a profusion of **Water Mint** and **Gipsywort**. The open shoreline has occasional plants of the exotically-named **Trifid Bur-marigold**.

Tufted Ducks

During early summer, male **Emperor Dragonflies,** with flashing blue tails patrol the pond margins on the lookout for rival males or potential mates. Later in the season, **Common Darters** stake a claim to this valuable territory.

Sinah Gravel Pit has no public access but can be viewed from the Gun Site open space adjacent to Ferry Road.

The Hampshire Wildlife Trust Reserve at Sinah

The first, ill-fated, construction scheme for the Hayling Billy Line envisaged the track being laid across Langstone Harbour to avoid the expense of buying land. Most of the embankments were soon washed away and the scheme was abandoned. One section still remains; a gravel bank extending across the harbour, north of the Kench. This shingle bank is used today by large numbers of roosting waders, gulls and terns. The material to construct this bank was dug from Sinah Common and the large depression left behind lies between Ferry Road and the golf course. This area is now managed by the Hampshire Wildlife Trust as a Nature Reserve.

The Hampshire Wildlife Trust Reserve floods during the winter. In summer it dries out allowing a number of scarce plants to flourish.

During winter, the reserve remains flooded and is used by ducks and the occasional Water Rail taking advantage of the thick fringing vegetation.

A form of dune slack vegetation has developed here with Creeping Willow, Dotted Sedge and **Royal Fern** at its only locality in south-east Hampshire. The area around the reserve is part of the golf course and supports a particularly fine stand of Bell Heather interspersed with Sheep's-bit. This is also one of the best places on Hayling for **Long** and **Short-winged Cone-head** and the very local Grey Bush-cricket.

Lakeside Holiday Centre Pool, Fishery Lane

The pool at the Lakeside Holiday Camp is the second largest body of fresh water on the Island. The pool has far less aquatic vegetation and surrounding scrub than Sinah Gravel Pit and has far higher levels of human disturbance. Despite this, the pool regularly holds a wintering flock of Tufted Duck and Pochard, and parties of Brent Geese frequently drop in to bathe. It is one of the best sites to see Little Grebes in the winter. **Moorhens** nest on the pool, unperturbed by the large numbers of visitors.

Tournerbury Farm Pond

Tournerbury Farm has always had a pond but the recent construction of a much larger one has led to the colonisation by several interesting new species. In summer Little Grebes breed amid a spectacular display of

The recent colonisation of Hayling Island by the Ruddy Darter may be due to an influx of continental migrants of this species which have established themselves on the island.

76

Fringed Water-lily . Dragonflies which have rapidly started to breed in this new pond include the **Ruddy Darter**. This scarce species has recently become established on Hayling, both at Tournerbury and Sinah Gravel Pit. Virtually all the species of plants and animals which live in fresh water have a stage of mobility in their life cycle,

While probably introduced to Hayling Island, Fringed Water-lily looks very much at home on the pond at Tournerbury Farm.

adaptations which enable them to exploit new areas. For example, plants have seeds dispersed by the wind and most insects can fly. Thus, new ponds are rapidly colonised and become havens for wildlife in a very short period of time.

Ditches

Hayling has an network of ditches, which drain rainwater into the harbours. On an island with few freshwater habitats these ditches are important refuges for wetland plants and animals. As its name suggests the towering **Hemlock Water-dropwort** is highly poisonous. Even a small amount of the plant's sap on your skin can cause painful blisters. **Wild Celery** is another member of the *Apiaceae* (formerly *Umbellifer*) family which grows in Hayling's damp ditches. Wild Celery is a scarce plant in Hampshire, restricted to coastal areas. It was from this species that cultivated celery was derived.

Daw Lane - the ditch to the north of the road once formed the parish boundary between north and south Hayling.

The oldest and deepest ditch on the island runs along Daw Lane. This ditch marked the historic boundary between the parishes of north and south Hayling. Hundreds of Primroses bloom along its banks in early spring.

Woodlands and Hedgerows

The caterpillars of White Admirals feed on Honeysuckle growing in shaded woodland. Tournerbury Wood is the only site on the island for this magnificent butterfly..

Hayling's original woodland was felled thousands of years ago by early human settlers and today the island remains relatively poorly wooded.

Those woodland plants and animals which do survive in small copses and hedgerows may well be the ancestors of some of the island's original inhabitants.

Tournerbury Wood

Situated on the site of a probable Iron Age fort and a Roman settlement, the earthworks at Tournerbury support the largest remaining woodland on the island. Towering **Oak** trees and ancient **Yews** growing above a water-filled moat add to the atmosphere of antiquity about the place. Many of the tallest Oaks within the earthworks contain the nests of Grey Herons. This is the only heronry on Hayling with about a dozen nests, and is said to have been here since Roman times.

Dennis Johnson

The sight of drifts of Bluebells on a woodland floor, such as here in Tournerbury, is a spectacle only seen in the British Isles. Bluebells are bulbs which thrive in our damp, maritime climate.

In recent years a sizeable roost of Little Egrets has developed in the wood raising hope that they may also nest in the near future.

In May, the floor of Tournerbury Wood is carpeted with **Bluebells,** a common enough sight on the mainland but one which has all but vanished from Hayling Island. Accompanying the Bluebells are the white flowers of **Greater Stitchwort** and the occasional **Red Campion** giving the spring-time wood a patriotic red, white and blue colouring. Plants of woodland rides such as **Betony, Wood Anemone, Wood Millet** and **Wood Speedwell** still grow in Tournerbury Wood long after their disappearance from the rest of Hayling.

Not surprisingly, Tournerbury is the best location on Hayling for woodland birds. Both Green Woodpecker and **Great Spotted Woodpecker,** breed here, and the elusive **Lesser Spotted Woodpecker** is seen occasionally. Other hole-nesting species such as **Stock Dove, Jackdaw** and **Starling** also add their voices to the dawn chorus of tits and finches. The mixture of broad-leaved and conifer trees encourages species like **Coal Tit** and **Goldcrest** which both nest here along with the island's only breeding **Treecreepers**. The arrival of summer migrants increases the variety of birdsong when **Blackcaps, Willow Warblers** and **Chiffchaffs** join the chorus.

In most years, Tournerbury is home to a pair of **Sparrowhawks** giving the ever-noisy Jackdaws something to complain about. **Tawny Owls** too, breed in the wood. Sometimes a roosting Tawny Owl will be discovered by the local small bird population. The unfortunate owl will then be mobbed and harassed until forced to find a quieter location usually deep among the branches of a Yew tree.

Dennis Johnson

The damp woodland rides contain a number of flowers such as **Primrose, Wood Spurge** and **Bugle** which are attractive to insects. In spring, **Green-veined Whites** and **Orange Tip** butterflies appear, patrolling the paths on the lookout for mates. **Speckled Wood** butterflies, while not restricted to woodland, are common in Tournerbury and can often be seen basking on patches of Bramble.

Great Spotted Woodpecker is the commonest of the three species of British woodpecker and can be seen and heard all over the island. They occasionally visit gardens to feed on peanuts.

By July, the flowers of Bramble are being used by **White Admiral** butterflies which glide gracefully through the clearings, in apparently effortless flight. Darting around the tops of the Oak trees are **Purple Hairstreaks**. These attractive little butterflies are actually quite common on Hayling, but due to their habit of spending most of their lives in the tree-tops they are rarely seen.

By mid-summer much of the woodland floor is covered with Bracken but, in sunny glades, **Woodland Grasshoppers** call at their only Hayling site.

Purple Hairstreaks live in colonies and spend their entire lives around the Oak trees on which their larvae feed.

A map of Hayling drawn in 1834 shows Tournerbury Wood as being restricted to the area of the circular earth works. At that time both North Copse on St. Peters Road and Farm Copse, north of the Manor House, were larger. Extensive 20th century planting, not least after the storms of 1987 and 1990, have extended Tournerbury Wood south to the shore of My Lords Pond. This new woodland contains many open glades and a large brackish pond which supports small populations of Sea Lavender and the scarce Sea Heath.

Tournerbury Wood is private property with no public access.

Most of North Copse was felled during 1944/45 for its valuable timber. Despite this, there are still many fine Oak trees alongside St. Peters Road and around the Broad Oak Hotel. These, and the

The ancient Yews at Tournerbury are thought to have been planted by monks in the 13th century.

splendid collection of Oaks scattered through the nearby caravan park, are the last surviving remnants of a once extensive woodland. Farm Copse too has largely disappeared, with only a relic population of old Oaks left around the buildings at Manor Farm.

Trees on shingle

At the eastern end of Sinah Gravel Pit a remarkable woodland has developed, growing in almost pure shingle. The wood consists mainly of scrub Oaks and Sallow trees and provides an attractive backdrop to the open water. In early spring, migrant Chiffchaffs hunt for insects amongst the Sallow blossom, disturbing the first Drone Flies of the year.

Being close to the gravel pit, the woodland provides rich pickings for recently emerged dragonflies and damselflies which hunt for small insects on the wing. In late summer hundreds of **Common Darters** and **Migrant Hawkers** can be seen hovering in sunny clearings between the Oak trees.

Common Darter

Saltmarsh Copse

Lying alongside the Hayling Billy Coastal Path are several small areas of woodland, the largest of which is known as 'Saltmarsh Copse'. The woodland here consists largely of Oak with an understorey of **Hawthorn, Holly, Ivy** and **Bramble.** The copse contains several species of plant which are indicators of ancient woodland including **Butcher's-broom** and **Stinking Iris.**

Firecrest - this scarce relative of the Goldcrest occurs on Hayling every autumn. A few remain to winter on the island.

Within the copse are a pond and a large borrow pit dug during the construction of the Billy Line. The borrow pit remains flooded for most of the year and has been invaded by Sallow and Common Reed. In recent years some of the large Sallows in the pit have been cut allowing more light in and producing areas of open water, ideal for breeding Moorhens.

There are old records of **Great Crested Newt** from the pit. These rare (and legally protected) amphibians may still be present.

This copse is home to breeding Great Spotted Woodpeckers, Blackcaps and a number of other common woodland birds. In some years it attracts wintering **Firecrests.**

Rookery Nook

In 1904, three circular areas of mixed woodland were planted at Northney Farm. A variety of native and non-native species were used in the planting and today these areas of woodland are a prominent feature of Northney. In spring and summer these tall trees resound with the constant noise of a large rookery.

Rooks nest colonially, usually in the canopy of tall trees. Remaining paired throughout the winter, Rooks return to their nests early in the year. By mid-February, the rookery is a hive of activity, birds bring in sticks to repair

Butcher's-broom

last year's nests and quarrel with their neighbours. The first eggs are laid in early March enabling the young to fledge before the ground is baked hard in summer preventing them from reaching their main food, earthworms.

Rook

Planted with the woodland at Northney were a line of poplars and **Scots Pines**. Scots Pine is one of only three species of conifer native to the British Isles. Following the last Ice Age Scots Pine would probably have covered large parts of southern England including Hayling, but today it only grows naturally in northern Scotland. Several insects which feed on pine, including the **Pine Hawkmoth** and the appropriately named **Grey Pine Carpet** moth, appear regularly in this part of the island.

Stoke Common Wood

To most Hayling residents Stoke Common Wood is the most visible woodland on the island. Situated next to Havant Road, north of the petrol station, the wood contains many fine Oak trees and is an impressive feature as you enter or leave the island. The woodland consists mainly of old boundary trees and a number of young Oaks and scrub which developed on the former Stoke Common after its enclosure in 1874.

Pine Hawkmoth

Orchards

Orchards have long been a feature of the island's landscape. Northney was at one time the centre of apple farming on Hayling and had a number of small orchards scattered round the village. Most of these orchards have long since gone, but many gardens in the area still retain some of the apple trees.

In more recent times, several large commercial orchards were planted along Daw Lane. To give the orchards some protection from the wind, rows of poplars were planted along their boundaries. Most of these orchards have

now been 'grubbed up', but
the poplars remain towering
over the much older Oak
trees next to them.

The loss of orchards has
deprived **Redwings,**
Fieldfares, Blackbirds, Song
and **Mistle Thrushes** of a
valuable food source because
any apples remaining after
the autumn harvest were left
on the ground. In hard weather, these old
apples attracted flocks of several hundred
thrushes.

Lombardy Poplars along St Peter's Road

Lombardy Poplars

Hayling is flat and coastal and therefore
prone to strong winds. During the last 100
years, the planting of lines of **Lombardy**
Poplars as wind-breaks has become
commonplace giving parts of the island
a French feel. One of the most
impressive rows was planted along St.
Peters Road around 70 years ago, but
many are post-war in origin.

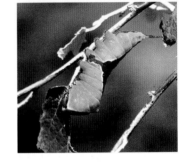

Hedgerows

Hedgerows are planted for a purpose,
sometimes as boundary markers or to
provide shelter but, most commonly, for confining livestock. Some hedges,
notably those around Woodgaston Lane, may well be ancient but many of
the island's hedges were planted during the 19th century. Made up largely of
Hawthorn, **Blackthorn** and Elm, these hedges were used both for confining
sheep and as cover for game. As shooting increased in popularity, many
hedges around the West Lane Fields were allowed to grow very wide in order
to provide cover for the large number of Grey and **Red-legged Partridges**
then found on the island.

Puss moth. The caterpillar (above) of this
species can be found feeding on poplar trees
during the summer.

Hedges were managed by periodic cutting or laying. This kept the base of
the hedge thick and stock proof but was very labour intensive. At intervals
along the hedge, trees, usually Oak or Elm, were allowed to grow to provide

timber and firewood for the farm. On Hayling you can see the ghost of old hedgerows in the lines of Oak trees spread across open arable fields, the hedges in which they once stood long since gone.

Hayling's summer hedgerows are often bordered with white-flowered **Cow Parsley** and **Garlic Mustard**. The latter species grows along many of the island's main roads. Rubbing the leaves releases a strong scent of garlic, but this does not deter Orange Tip butterflies whose caterpillars feed on the seed pods.

The tragedy of the Elm
Old photographs of Hayling tell their own story of how important **Elm** trees were to the landscape of the island. Tall and elegant, these magnificent trees were ravaged by the scourge of Dutch elm disease.

Elms do not set viable seed in this country but sucker along a hedgerow as a series of identical plants. These suckers are easy to gather and were widely used in the planting of new hedges. The result is that an entire hedge may be made up of plants derived from a single

The summer of 2000 saw many Elms on Hayling succumb to a new bout of Dutch elm disease. These trees along West Lane were about 30 years old.

tree. The large Elm hedges around the Maypole Pub may well have been planted in this fashion. Lack of genetic diversity results in vulnerability to disease. If one tree becomes infected, they all suffer. This may explain why following the recent recurrence of Dutch elm disease, the island's hedges seem filled with rows of identical skeletons.

The fatal fungi is carried from tree to tree by the **Elm Bark Beetle**. Young trees do not seem to attract the beetle and remain immune from the disease. Once trees reach about 30 years of age they become susceptible and rapidly die. Many of Hayling's Elms were suckers from trees killed in the 1970s epidemic and have reached this vulnerable age. Sadly, in the last couple of years (1999-2000) large-scale death of Elms has returned to Hayling. It may be that full-grown Elm trees will never again grace the island.

Hedgerow wildlife along the Coastal Path

Some of the best and most easily accessible hedgerow wildlife on the island can be found along the Hayling Billy Coastal Path. A spring or summer walk along the Coastal Path should reveal some of this wildlife.

In our farmed landscape denuded of trees, hedgerows are an important refuge for resident birds such as **Robin, Dunnock** (or **Hedge Sparrow**) and **Yellowhammer**. **Long-tailed Tits** often breed in hedges, building their extraordinary nests in dense tangles of Gorse.

Whitethroats are summer visitors, announcing their arrival with a loud scratchy song often uttered in hovering display flights. **Turtle Doves** are one of the last summer migrants to return from Africa. By June their soft churring call can be heard

Dennis Johnson

Long-tailed Tits construct remarkable nests from moss and lichen held together with spiders' silk and lined with hundreds of feathers.

from thick banks of Blackthorn next to the line. Turtle Doves are hard to see as they usually sit below the top of a bush just out of sight. The thick scrub along the line also offers the best chance of a singing **Nightingale**. Despite a

Hayling Billy Coastal Path

The Hayling Billy Line, linking Havant and Hayling Island, was opened on 17 July 1867. The line operated profitably until its closure in 1963 when the cost of replacing the timber bridge carrying it to the mainland was considered too high. Twenty years of dereliction followed before the route of the old line was converted into a footpath and bridleway.

The Hayling Billy Coastal Path is now managed by the County Council's Countryside Service. The path provides excellent opportunities for observing the wildlife of Langstone Harbour. The shingle bank at Knotts Marsh has a fine stand of **Sea Campion** and encloses a rich area of salt marsh where **Sea Arrowgrass** and Sea Purslane occur. There are several ancient meadows to the east of the line, and a series of hedgerows and woodlands alongside, which give Hayling a wooded appearance from Langstone Harbour.

decline in numbers nationally, Nightingales occasionally take up residence and serenade late night walkers with their fluid musical song.

April brings the snow-white blossom of Blackthorn, followed in May by the heady scent of Hawthorn. Flowering Gorse and **Honeysuckle** vie with **Dog Rose** and climbing **Tufted Vetch** as the hedgerows burst into colour.

Turtle Dove

Hawthorn was widely planted in hedges as its thorny branches are stock proof.
In May, white Hawthorn blossom blankets the hedgerow giving it the country name 'May'.

Elder bushes thrive along the Billy Line as they seem very tolerant of salt spray. The sweet-scented summer flowers give rise to vast numbers of Elderberries in autumn which are eagerly consumed by hoards of young Starlings and migrant warblers. Blackberry bushes heavy with fruit are attractive to birds and humans alike. At night they are raided by **Wood Mice** which venture into the hedgerow drawn by this short-lived harvest. The numerous young rabbits in the hedges attract hunting **Weasels**.

Abundant bramble flowers attract hedgerow butterflies including the **Gatekeeper** (or **Hedge Brown**), **Large Skipper** and occasionally **Wall Browns**. A wide variety of insects live in the hedgerow but most go unseen. In late summer **Dark Bush-cricket, Oak Bush-cricket** and **Speckled Bush-cricket** are all found here. The nocturnal chirp of Dark Bush-crickets is a familiar sound on warm summer nights.

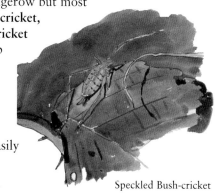

Autumn dew picks out the webs of **Garden Orb-spiders** cast between the branches. These common spiders are easily recognised by the white cross on their abdomens.

Speckled Bush-cricket

Farmland

Man has been farming on Hayling Island for several thousand years and his activities have greatly modified the landscape and its associated wildlife.

Initial small clearances in the 'wildwood' were gradually enlarged until the island was predominantly agricultural. Since Roman times, Hayling's combination of highly fertile brickearth soil, mild winters and hot summers has been recognised as excellent for growing crops. In 1939, land at north Hayling produced the highest yield of wheat per acre in the whole of England!

Common Poppy

For thousands of years plants which had previously been confined to woodland clearings flourished in the new open landscape. **Common Poppy, Common Cornsalad, Corn Marigold** and **Common Fumitory** are all examples of plants which followed man out into the fields. These annual plants survived within the crops and were often a considerable nuisance to the farmer. With the advent of modern herbicides, the populations of these arable weeds on Hayling, as elsewhere, went into drastic decline. Some arable weeds are now amongst the most endangered wild plants in Britain. Today, arable fields support few wild plants, even the red splash of Common Poppies in summer fields has become a rare sight.

Farmland at Lower Tye Farm.

Recent changes in policy towards farming hold out some hope for plants of arable land. The establishment of wider field margins, land set aside from production and a reduction in the amount of herbicides used are all beneficial. Let's hope that soon these attractive 'weeds' will be creeping back along field margins helping to enliven a walk in the country.

Farmland birds benefit when stubble fields are left unploughed during the winter. Mixed flocks of finches and buntings gather to feed on discarded seeds. Linnets, Greenfinches and Yellowhammers concentrate in the few fields where food is available. In the past, flocks of **Tree Sparrows** and **Corn Buntings** were also a regular sight on Hayling. Both are now rarities on the island, victims of modern farming methods where stubble is ploughed and new seed is sown in the autumn.

The Turtle Dove is a summer visitor which feeds mainly on weed seeds, especially those of fumitory.

One bird which has definitely benefited from the farmed environment is the Brent Goose. Brent Geese like to graze on modern fertilized pastures which provide a rich source of nourishment throughout the winter. Grassland suffers little long term damage but if the geese move onto winter cereal crops the combination of grazing and trampling can be detrimental. Every year, farmers on Hayling try a range of devices to keep the geese off their crops with varying degrees of success.

Yellowhammer

Golden Plover and Lapwing feed on farmland as do Curlew and even Oystercatchers. In northern England and Scotland, Oystercatchers are just as much a bird of the fields as they are of the coast. Oystercatchers often breed far inland feeding on earthworms and other invertebrates.

A large part of Hayling Island consists of farmland. In the past this land would have been home to a wide variety of wildlife. Economic pressures have forced farmers to produce food in a more and more intensive fashion, leaving much of today's farmland virtually devoid of life. It seems, at last, that politicians and consumers have woken up to the demise of farmland wildlife. Let's hope it has a brighter future.

Hayling's 'chalk downs'

Much of the northern half of the island has a bedrock of chalk but this is overlain by a thick layer of brickearth and cannot be seen at the surface.

During the construction of the railway line in the 1860s, large amounts of quarried chalk were brought onto Hayling to build an embankment across marshland at the northern end of the island. Today, the busy railway is only a memory but the chalk banks remain supporting a group of plants and animals found nowhere else on the island and more typical of chalk downland on the mainland.

Downland supports a richer flora than any other habitat in Great Britain. A stroll along the section of the line adjacent to the old Oysterbeds in high summer gives a flavour of this diversity. Rising from the thin chalk soil is the elegant Yellow-wort, its blue-green leaves wrapped distinctively round its stem topped by a cluster of lemon yellow flowers. Surprisingly difficult to spot amongst the grass are the flower spikes of **Bee Orchids**, while less showy species like **Kidney Vetch, Bladder Campion** and **Fairy Flax** are also strong indicators of a chalky soil. A plant, scarce in Hampshire but with a thriving colony on these banks is the Spiny Restharrow, its large pink and white flowers indicate its membership of the pea family. This, and its close relative **Common Restharrow,** get their name from their deep roots which were said to be able to stop a horse-drawn harrow in its tracks, leading them to be regarded as serious agricultural weeds.

Spiny Restharrow

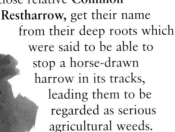

Marbled White

The multiple flower heads of **Greater Knapweed** and **Marjoram** are highly attractive to butterflies. On hot summer days, swarms of Gatekeepers and

Yellow-wort

Great Green Bush-cricket - a female laying her eggs in the soil.

Meadow Browns patrol the banks alongside **Marbled Whites**, a species which has recently colonised the island and is usually associated with the downs.

On warm, late summer evenings, the strident call of **Great-green Bush-crickets** can be heard along the line and in some nearby hedgerows. This, the largest of the British bush-crickets, can grow to 8cm in length and is always an impressive sight as it clambers deftly around the vegetation.

A tropical looking insect on the northern edge of its range on the south coast of the British Isles, the Great Green Bush-cricket occurs commonly on Portsdown Hill but is found nowhere else on Hayling.

One of the main threats to chalk downland is scrub invasion when woody species gradually take over, smothering out the classic rich assemblage of flowering plants. On Hayling too, this threat exists with **Dogwood** and **Privet** both spreading along the sides of the embankment. Some control of these species is necessary to help maintain the open areas. A more serious long-term problem is the gradual erosion of the banks by the waters of Langstone Harbour, a process which has been going on since they were originally constructed and which if left unchecked, will eventually destroy this botanically rich corner of the island.

Bee Orchid

Gardens

The total area of gardens in Britain is far larger than the total area of Nature Reserves.

As the agricultural landscape becomes more intensively farmed, gardens are increasingly important as refuges for wildlife.

Garden Ponds
Wide-scale infilling of ponds in the countryside has reduced the habitat available to wetland wildlife such as amphibians and aquatic insects. Garden ponds have now become vital to many of these species.

Garden ponds are rich wildlife habitats.

The amphibians, **Common Frog, Common Toad, Smooth** and **Palmate Newts** are frequently found in garden ponds on the island. In recent years a number of orange-coloured Common Frogs have been found. These appear to be at no disadvantage and will readily mate with individuals of normal colouring.

New ponds are rapidly colonised by aquatic insects. Some seem to take up residence almost while the pond is being filled! One of the early colonisers is the **Broad-bodied Chaser** dragonfly. The larva of this spectacular insect lives in the pond and is a ferocious predator, even tackling small fish.

Many garden lawns, especially around older houses, will have a good range of flowering plants growing in them. If cutting is ceased for a period many of these species will flower making a highly attractive spectacle. **Common Daisy** and **Selfheal** are both familiar plants of lawns while more unusual species can turn up. On Hayling Island, Common Spotted Orchid, Green-winged Orchid and Autumn Lady's-tresses have all appeared miraculously in islander's lawns, sometimes in abundance.

Male Smooth (above) and Palmate Newt.

92

Some seafront gardens lie on what was once open common land. The lawns here can be remarkably rich in Sea Pink, Sea Campion and Bird's-foot-trefoil. The soil is too poor to grow 'proper' grass so with a little care these natural flower gardens should be enjoyed for many years to come.

Many butterflies are more often seen in gardens than the wider countryside. Attracted by the range of exotic flowering plants, some species seem to specialise in these man-made environments. Plants such as *Buddleia* (Butterfly-bush), **Hebe** and **Iceplant** are irresistible to **Small Tortoiseshells, Peacocks** and **Red Admirals**. In some years, Painted Ladies join them, jostling on the flowerheads.

While many people enjoy seeing Small Tortoiseshells and Peacocks in their gardens, they are less keen on the foodplant of their caterpillars, **Stinging Nettles**. The loss of untidy nettle patches from gardens and rough ground is one reason for the decline in the numbers of these vibrant, gaudy butterflies.

Around Northney, **Wild Hop** can be seen scrambling over hedgerows and scrub banks, its long vines sometimes reaching to over 7 metres in length. These Hops are often planted in gardens where they are cultivated for the distinctive scent of the female flowers. Hop is the preferred foodplant for caterpillars of the **Comma** butterfly.

The spiky, white-backed caterpillars of the Comma resemble bird droppings, but can easily be found on the undersides of leaves. The Comma is one of the few butterflies to over-winter as an adult, emerging in early spring to seek a mate. It is regularly encountered in gardens all over Hayling, but this has not always been the case.

Comma. The name 'Comma' comes from the white comma-shaped mark on the underside of the wings.

The Comma has undergone a remarkable change in fortune during the last 100 years. At the beginning of the 20th century it was virtually extinct in England, being confined to the Welsh borders. Since then it has re-established itself over most of southern Britain and is now fairly common in a range of habitats.

Gardens are often the favoured haunt of the **Holly Blue** butterfly. This is the first of the 'blue' butterflies to emerge in spring. Adults fly around the tops of Holly bushes, even taking to the variegated forms often found in gardens. Holly Blues of the spring generation usually lay their eggs on the flowerbuds of Holly, while the second, midsummer generation prefer Ivy flowers.

The number of Holly Blues fluctuates wildly. In 1990 and 1991 they were one of the commonest butterflies on Hayling with every suitable bush colonised. In the years 1992/1994 they all but disappeared from the island. It appears that these huge fluctuations are partly due to a parasitic wasp which preys solely on the caterpillars of Holly Blues.

Honesty is widely planted in gardens for its attractive seeds, it will sometimes be used by egg-laying Orange Tip butterflies.

Stag Beetles

The Stag Beetle is one of the largest British insects, the males are 7cm in length including their huge antler-like jaws. Although fearsome looking, they are unable to bite people. The females have much smaller jaws but are capable of delivering a nip.

Although Stag Beetles have been declining in number in recent years, Hayling remains a stronghold for them. They can be seen from May to July and fly at night when they are often attracted to light. Gardens provide a suitable habitat for these beetles. The larvae spend up to four years feeding on rotting wood and have been found in log piles, rotting fence posts and dead roots of lilac and *Buddleia* bushes. Leaving some dead wood in your garden is a good way to encourage this magnificent insect.

Dennis Johnson

Feeding birds in the garden is a very popular activity. Millions of pounds are spent each year on bird seed and peanuts as people try to attract the local **Blue Tits, Great Tits, Chaffinches** and Robins to their birdtables. Feeding birds helps sustain them through cold weather when natural food is hard to come by. The artificially high numbers of small birds in gardens attracts predators. Sparrowhawks are regular visitors to gardens and are always in the top 20 in the RSPB survey of the most regularly seen garden birds.

Dennis Johnson

Chaffinches can be attracted to gardens by providing wild bird seed.

Blue Tits and Great Tits are woodland birds, nesting in holes. Lack of suitable nesting sites means they readily turn to nest boxes provided in gardens.

Gardens provide some of the best opportunities for observing wild mammals. **Foxes** are now found all over Hayling and strongly divide local opinion. To some people the fox is an attractive animal, welcome, or even encouraged, into their garden; to others it is a nocturnal, dustbin-raiding pest.

Dennis Johnson

Foxes have adapted well to man-made environments such as gardens.

Less controversial are **Hedgehogs** which can frequently be heard snuffling their way around suburban gardens in search of worms and slugs. Bats have been little studied on Hayling, but with the island's dearth of woodland and freshwater habitats, the range of species is probably limited. One species which is regularly seen is the **Pipistrelle**, a small bat usually encountered hawking over gardens on warm summer evenings.

Collared Doves first appeared in Britain in 1955 when they colonised Norfolk. In 1961 they bred on Hayling Island, the first place in Hampshire. They are now frequent visitors to gardens, where they regularly nest.

Churchyards

Churchyards may seem strange places to look for wildlife, but many have remained untouched by modern herbicides and retain a rich flora. The churchyards of both St Mary's and St Peter's on Hayling have many wild flowers growing between the headstones. These natural gardens seem a fitting tribute to the dearly departed.

Yew Trees

Yew trees have a long association with churchyards. The Yew was taken from pagan mythology to become a Christian symbol of immortality. On Hayling, St Peter's, at Northney has several venerable old Yew trees, but the oldest and largest on the island is in St Mary's churchyard. At 10 metres, this tree apparently has the largest girth of any Yew in Hampshire. Probably well over 1000 years old, the tree would have been here long before the church, which was built in the 13th century. The presence of this Yew tree may therefore have been significant in the siting of the church.

Yew berries

Yew trees prefer to grow on well-drained chalk or limestone soil so may not have been present on the island in the original 'wildwood'. Widely planted for their wood and mythical associations, Yew trees are now found all over lowland Britain.

Despite their legendary antiquity, accurate determination of the age of Yew trees is difficult. With advancing years the tree becomes hollow, losing the growth rings normally used for ageing. The Yew's foliage is highly poisonous to livestock and has often been responsible for the deaths of sheep and cattle. The seeds are also poisonous, but not the surrounding red arils which are eagerly consumed by birds. Thrushes seem particularly fond of Yew berries and a large tree will sometimes attract a noisy mixed flock of Blackbirds, Redwings and Fieldfares.

Redwing

Lichens

Hayling has no natural outcrops of rock so species such as lichens, which grow on rock surfaces, have turned to man-made structures instead. Generally, older stone buildings such as churches have a wider variety of lichen species growing on them.

Of the 1600 species of lichen in the British Isles, no fewer than 600 have been found in churchyards. Winchester Cathedral for instance has over 100 species of lichen growing on it. The church walls and headstones at St Peter's are particularly attractive with their multi-coloured coating of lichens giving a mellow, weathered appearance to the stone.

Lichens on gravestone

The scarce maritime lichen *Roccella phycopsis* grows on St Mary's Church tower. This species is normally only found on sea cliffs in south-west England. On Hayling it appears to use the damp stone of the north side of the tower as a surrogate sea cliff.

The island's oldest resident

Lying almost forgotten in a bramble hedge next to Mill Rythe School is a large boulder.

Washed out from vast ice sheets 75,000 years ago, these rocks once littered the whole island. With no natural rock on Hayling these boulders made tempting building materials. They were used in the construction of St Mary's and St Peter's churches. Today, this is the last of these rocks of any size left *in situ* on the island, a link with Hayling's distant past.

Plants with a History

Hayling is rich in plant life. Indeed, it is the most important area of Hampshire for the maritime vegetation of beaches and dunes. Some of these plants have an added significance in that they are either nationally rare or have an historic connection with the island.

Sea Knotgrass is a low-growing, long-lived perennial which develops a woody stem as it gets older. Its small white flowers are carried for a prolonged period, sometimes from June right through to November.

Sea Knotgrass, a Mediterranean plant on the northern edge of its range, thought to have been extinct in Britain since 1902. Growing just above the strand line on sand and shingle beaches, its rediscovery in the UK in 1990 was a notable botanical event. Severe storms apparently uncovered some of its remarkably resilient seed which germinated when exposed to the light. Over the next few years, the plant appeared at several localities along the south coast and in 1995, was found at Sandy Point, Hayling. The initial discovery was of just 15 plants, but these have now grown to number several hundred, the largest colony in Britain. The main threat to its survival now appears to be from trampling by people unaware of the rarity beneath their feet.

Childing Pink was for many years the lost jewel of Hayling's plant life. Formerly abundant on the vegetated shingle at the west end of Sinah Common, the colony was destroyed by development in the 1920s, the last plant being seen on the site of what is now the Havant Borough Car Park in 1928.

Since the 1960s, the only site in Britain for this attractive plant had been Pagham Harbour in West Sussex where it grows on a vulnerable shingle spit.

A chance discovery in 1998 of several Childing Pink flowers on an area of Beachlands well away from the original colony has reconnected the island to part of its botanical heritage and given the species a valuable second British location. Careful management work by Beachlands staff and the Hampshire Wildlife Trust will hopefully assist the colony to grow.

Deptford Pink (left) and Childing Pink (right).

A second member of the 'Pink' family was also once resident on Hayling Island. A large colony of **Deptford Pink** was known from Sinah Common where it grew on rough ground near the ferry. This beautiful, dark-pink flowered species appears to have been lost to the island due to a combination of development and invasion by rank vegetation, the last known sighting being in 1981. Sadly, Deptford Pink has declined rapidly and is now found in little more than a dozen sites throughout the country. The rediscovery of Childing Pink on Hayling offers some hope that Deptford Pink too may one day reappear to grace the island.

Sea Heath bears its delicate pink flowers in late summer emerging from trailing branches, each covered with the fine 'heather-like' leaves from which it gets its name.

Sea Heath, a tough, mat-forming, little plant which likes to grow in the 'no-mans land' between salt marsh and shingle has had a long association with Hayling.

At the northern limit of its European range, the first ever British record of Sea Heath came from Hayling Island in 1621. Today, it remains the only place in Hampshire where it grows. Previously found in only a single location on the island, a new site was discovered in 2000 helping to safeguard the long term-future of Haylings unsung 'floral emblem.'

Alien Invaders

Many of Hayling's most distinctive animals and plants do not occur here naturally but have been introduced either accidentally or deliberately by man. The stories behind some of these introductions offer a fascinating insight into the island's history.

Plants from Far and Wide

Hayling's mild climate has enabled some species to survive that would perish elsewhere. The sandy soils of Gunner Point and the golf course play host to **Tree Lupins** whose magnificent towers of sweet-scented yellow blossom are admired by locals and visitors alike.

Tree Lupins on the dunes at Sinah Common.

The species originates from California and can spread with prodigious speed, rapidly taking over large areas and presenting a real problem to the golf course groundsmen. Luckily, it seems to be in a kind of natural balance with a large species of aphid (also introduced) which attacks and rapidly kills the bushes when numbers become too high. A few plants survive each major 'die off' and gradually restock the area until the cycle is repeated.

Carpeting the ground over many areas of Beachlands is another New World import, **Spring Beauty**. A distinctive plant, its white flowers emerge from the middle of a round leaf, it was first recorded in this country at the end of the 19th century. The sandy soil of south Hayling appears much to its liking and it seems to have taken up permanent residence there.

Hoary Bittercress

A notorious addition to the British flora is **Hoary Bittercress** also known as Portsmouth Weed. A white-flowered member of the cabbage family, this highly invasive perennial is very difficult to eradicate and will rapidly colonise sand dunes, waste ground and gardens. Its roots may grow to a depth of 3 metres so, inevitably, part of the root is always left in the ground after digging. First appearing in 1809, Hoary Bittercress was introduced to Britain by accident in an unusual fashion. Its seeds arrived in mattresses brought back by soldiers returning from the French wars. A farmer in Kent used the hay from the bedding as manure and the seeds germinated. Since then it has spread along the south coast and is now a common sight all over Hayling.

Some plants have been deliberately introduced to do a specific job. **Tamarisk** is a shrub native to North Africa and south-west Europe. Tolerant of salt spray and able to survive in areas with very little water, it has proved ideal as a coastal wind break and for stabilising mobile shingle beaches.

Widely planted along the south coast, Hayling has some fine stands of Tamarisk particularly at the western end of the golf course on the approach to Gunner Point. Interestingly in recent years a continental moth, the **Channel Islands Pug,** which feeds on Tamarisk, has become established on Hayling, the first place in Britain to be colonised.

Large-flowered Evening-primrose

The sand dunes at Sandy Point come alive in late summer with the yellow trumpets of **Large-flowered Evening-primrose**. Long after most native plants have finished flowering this attractive North American species adds a splash of colour. A 19th century introduction, it is now widely naturalised in southern Britain.

Species which occur naturally elsewhere in Britain have also been introduced to Hayling Island. **Tree Mallow** is a spectacular shrub capable of growing 3 metres high, with purple-veined, rose-pink flowers. Native on south-western coastlines of Great Britain, it proved irresistible to gardeners who transplanted it to Hayling. Escaping readily from cultivation it has become well-established on waste ground along the island's seafront and at Sandy Point.

Emerging from a raft of leaves, the beautiful yellow flowers of Fringed Water-lily grace many of the island's ponds. In Britain, Fringed Water-lily is probably truly native only in East Anglia but has been widely introduced as an ornamental species. It spreads rapidly to new waters on the feet of wildfowl.

Rose Campion is a garden escape, which grows freely on Gunner Point, the only site in the county where this attractive alien has become established.

Animals and Birds
Hayling has its fair share of non-native animals. Some, such as the **Hare,** introduced for food by the Romans and the **Rabbit,** brought back by crusaders in the 12th century, are long-standing imports. A more recent, and not altogether welcome, addition is the **Grey Squirrel** from North America. It appears that Hayling resisted the invasion of this arboreal vandal until very recent times, when it was apparently introduced deliberately!

Several of our most familiar species of bird also have their origins elsewhere. The **Canada Geese** which breed on the island are from North America. Introduced into Britain in the 18th century they have flourished in their adopted country. Noisy skeins can be heard flying overhead at any time of year and their numbers on the island are still increasing.

Hailing from the other side of the world the **Ring-necked Pheasant** was introduced, probably by the Normans, as a quarry species for hunting. Large numbers of Pheasants are still reared for shooting each year around Tournerbury Wood.

Perhaps a more surprising introduction is that of the **Little Owl.** It was the owl's diet of small rodents and insects which persuaded the Victorians that it would be a useful addition to our countryside for 'controlling unwanted pests'. It took many attempts over a 50 year period before the owls became firmly established in this country, but now to see one sitting in a West Lane Oak tree you would never know they were such a recent addition to the island's birdlife.

Grey Squirrel. This species has been introduced from North America.

Accidental introductions to Hayling include the **Slipper Limpet,** a species familiar to many islanders but with a little-known life history. Imported with North American Oysters in the 1880s, Slipper Limpets are now the dominant species in the animal community on the bed of the Solent. So common are they in the waters off Hayling Island that their empty shells form some of the beaches along the entrance to Langstone Harbour. Slipper Limpets have extraordinary reproductive behaviour. Piles of up to a dozen individuals live on top of each other, females at the bottom and the younger males at the top. As they grow Slipper Limpets change sex from male to female, so in each pile the males at the top fertilize the females below. It is not unusual to find groups of Slipper Limpets washed up on the beach still connected together.

Slipper Limpet shells

Swamp Cat

In July 1988, a Swamp Cat (*Felis chaus*) was killed by a car on West Lane. How it came to be there is a mystery as this wild cat is normally found in Egypt, the Middle East and Asia. At the time no Swamp Cats were known in captivity in the UK.

Photo courtesy of The Hayling Islander

Conservation

Hayling Island is adjacent to the Chichester Harbour Area of Outstanding Natural beauty (AONB) and is of great importance to wildlife. The harbours on either side of the island are of international significance for the habitats and the species they contain. The island itself has several nationally important plant communities as well as a range of sites valuable in a county context. Due to the range of highly important wildlife sites, it is not surprising that a number of organisations are actively involved in conservation on or around Hayling Island.

The government body responsible for safeguarding England's wildlife heritage is English Nature. Its role is to advise on and enforce legislation protecting our most threatened and important wildlife sites and species. It is English Nature which designates Sites of Special Scientific Interest (SSSI) such as that at Sinah Common. New European legislation also applies to many of the habitats around the island thereby expanding the role of English Nature.

The Hampshire Wildlife Trust (HWT) is a charity that owns and manages land throughout the county. The Trust has a small nature reserve on Hayling Island at Sinah Common. The reserve, owned by the Golf Course but managed by HWT, contains a number of scarce plants.

Areas of Wildlife Importance on Hayling

The Royal Society for the Protection of Birds (RSPB) has over one million members, including many on Hayling Island. The RSPB has no land on Hayling but does own and manage the islands in the north of Langstone Harbour where many of Hayling's seabirds breed. A summer warden is employed to monitor and protect the seabird colony during the breeding season.

All intertidal areas in harbours are SSSIs.

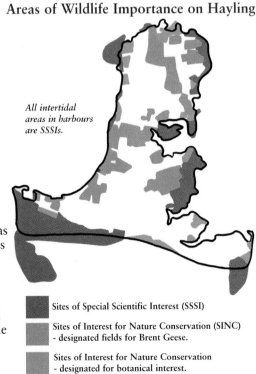

Hampshire County Council was one of the first local authorities in the country to take on the role of buying and managing land for its conservation and landscape importance. The County Council has purchased land on Hayling Island with the aim of safeguarding valuable natural assets for future generations.

Sites of Special Scientific Interest (SSSI)

Sites of Interest for Nature Conservation (SINC) - designated fields for Brent Geese.

Sites of Interest for Nature Conservation - designated for botanical interest.

104

The Local Nature Reserves at Sandy Point and the Kench are owned and managed by the County Council, along with the Hayling Billy Coastal Path and the fine salt marsh and mudflats at Gutner Point.

Havant Borough Council own a great deal of land on Hayling Island including most of the Beachlands area and the Hayling Oysterbeds. Working in partnership with English Nature and the Wildlife Trust, Havant BC is managing much of the new SSSI at Beachlands, including work to safeguard the future of the rare Childing Pink. The recent appointment of a part-time warden for the Hayling Oysterbeds has demonstrated a long-term commitment to this valuable site.

Langstone Harbour Board is the body responsible for the day-to-day running of Langstone Harbour, including safety of navigation, channel marking and moorings. A recent revision of the powers of the Harbour Board give it an expanded role, it is now involved in planning and development issues on land adjacent to the harbour as well as in the harbour itself. The creation of a new post, Assistant Harbour Master, with responsibility for the environment of the harbour, is an indication of how new legislation is pushing the environment higher up the agenda of many statutory bodies.

Chichester Harbour Conservancy was established by Act of Parliament in 1971. The conservancy has similar responsibilities to those of the Langstone Harbour Board, but also has a wider role in safeguarding the wildlife of the harbour and its surroundings, including land on the east shore of Hayling Island. The conservancy employs a full-time conservation officer whose responsibilities include organising a range of survey work and practical conservation projects.

Hayling is a small island with a growing human population of over 20,000. In the past, developments have often taken little account of the special wildlife present on the island. This was not due to malicious intent on the part of the landowner, but often through a lack of knowledge of the island's wildlife. Most of the incredibly rich heathland and grassland communities once found along the south coast of the island has been lost or damaged. However, pockets still remain, either protected within the nature reserve at Sandy Point or as part of Beachlands SSSI.

The public ownership of Beachlands, while not designed to protect rare habitats, has largely prevented the urbanisation so visible along Portsea Island and parts of the West Sussex coast.

The growth in the number of people belonging to conservation charities is an indication of the popularity wildlife enjoys. There is still much to cherish on Hayling Island. Most of the remaining areas of high wildlife value have some degree of protection, yet their long-term future may well be out of our hands as the inexorable rise of the sea may have the last word.

Sea-pink at Sinah Common.

The Future

The future for much of Hayling's wildlife is tied, as it has been for so long, to the actions of man. Pressure on the island's land resources for property development and food production are unlikely to diminish, but improved planning controls and long overdue change in agricultural policies are starting to bear fruit.

For both people and wildlife living on a low-lying island, one issue is set to dominate the next 100 years and beyond, sea level rise. Sea levels have generally been rising since the end of the last Ice Age but this has not occurred at a constant rate. During medieval times, a prolonged pause saw the growth of salt marshes around the island. The large salt marsh complex at Gutner Point was probably formed during this time. These salt marshes were often reclaimed for grazing land but this process proved only temporary. There is evidence that an extensive area of low-lying land to the south of Hayling was submerged between the 10th and 14th centuries.

The present pulse of sea level rise probably began in the 19th century and is almost certainly being hastened by man-induced climate change. Increased levels of carbon dioxide in the atmosphere prevent heat from the sun escaping leading to 'global warming'. Gradually rising temperatures worldwide cause the ice caps to melt, releasing long-stored water, resulting in higher sea levels. In the Solent, this problem is particularly acute. Rising sea levels combined with geological movements results in an annual rise of around 5mm, the highest rate anywhere around the UK coastline.

Salt marshes are capable of growing at 2mm in height per year, but are unable to keep pace with the current rate of sea level rise. Erosion, combined with the die back of *Spartina* has lead to a steady narrowing of Erosion on the west Hayling shore. the intertidal zone.
Removal of this natural sea defence has left sections of Hayling's coastline vulnerable to wave action.

In a totally natural situation the shape of the island would adapt, as it has before, in response to changing water levels. New areas of mudflats form as land is flooded and the line of high tide moves inland. For many centuries however, man has been 'resisting' the sea by the construction of sea walls and elaborate defences. Now, as levels rise, there is 'nowhere to go' for the mudflats and their associated bird and animal life. They are literally being squeezed between water and land.

For the internationally important assemblage of birds which use the harbours around Hayling each year, this process is potentially disastrous. Since 1870 the area of mudflats in the Solent has shrunk by 30 per cent, a huge loss in potential feeding area. If, as seems likely, this trend continues, by the middle of this century loss of habitat could drastically effect wintering bird numbers.

Gradually larger and larger areas will remain below water throughout the tidal cycle fundamentally altering the nature of Hayling Island's wildlife.

One proposed solution to this problem is the controversial idea of 'managed retreat'. Selected areas are allowed to flood, thereby creating new salt marsh which forms both a natural sea defence and good quality habitat for wildlife. This idea is understandably unpopular amongst some landowners but it also raises problems for conservationists.

The criteria by which land is selected for managed retreat often identify low-grade, coastal grazing land as ideally suitable due to its low economic value. Many of these areas on Hayling, such as those at Tournerbury and Middle Marshes, are SSSI (Sites of Special Scientific Interest) due to their rich flora. Any inundation by the sea in these areas would destroy one type of important habitat while replacing it with another.

As can be seen from this example the problems which face the residents of Hayling and those charged with protecting the natural environment are complex and have no single or easy solution.

It is to be hoped that what remains of Hayling's rich wildlife legacy will be safeguarded and enhanced by future generations. With the growth of 'green tourism' the wildlife which surrounds us may be seen to have important economic, as well as scientific value.

How we respond to the challenge of conserving vulnerable and fragile habitats in the future will go a long way to defining the quality of life on Hayling Island.

Viper's-bugloss

Where to see the Wildlife of Hayling Island

This month-by-month guide tells you where and when you can go to see much of the wildlife referred to in this book.

The sites mentioned in this section are all on Hayling Island. Some areas such as the Sandy Point and Gutner Point Nature Reserves, can only be accessed on guided walks or special events. Details of how to see these areas are included.

The best map of the island is *Ordnance Survey Explorer* Series 120 which marks all footpaths and parking areas. Ordnance Survey references are used to indicate locations.

Map showing locations of sites referred to in text.

Langstone Bridge

North Common

Rookery Nook

Stoke and Creek Common

Hayling Oysterbeds

Northney

St Peter's Church

St Peter's Road

Knott's Marsh

Woodgaston Lane

Langstone Harbour

West Lane Fields

Lower Tye Farm

Maypole Pub

Daw Lane

Verner Common

Gutner Point

Chichester Harbour

Billy Line

Mill Rythe

Manor Farm

Middle Marsh

Mulberry Harbour

Saltmarsh Copse

St Mary's Church

Tournerbury Marsh

The Kench

Sinah Warren

Tournerbury Wood

HWT Nature Reserve

Sinah Gravel Pit

West Town

Mengham

My Lords Pond

Black Point

Sinah Common

Beachlands

Lakeside Holiday Centre

Gunner Point

East Winner

Hayling Bay

Sandy Point

The Solent

108

January

Most of these suggestions would apply equally well to any of the winter months.

Hayling Oysterbeds (see page 16)
Timing: Best time to visit is usually on a rising tide 1-2 hours before high tide.
Species: Large roost of waders including: *Dunlin, Oystercatcher, Redshank* and *Ringed Plover*. Also good for wildfowl with *Brent Geese, Red-breasted Merganser, Goldeneye* and *Shelduck* in the lagoons. Both *Merlin* and *Peregrine* are regular here hunting the wader roost. If you have a telescope, try looking in Langstone Harbour for ducks and grebes including *Great Crested Grebe* and *Black-necked Grebe*.
Access: Can be reached from the Havant BC car park behind the Esso Garage at SU 717029.

Black Point (see page 12)
Timing: High tide for seabirds, low/rising tide for waders.
Species: The harbour entrance is a good spot for *Great Northern Diver*, Grebes and Auks. The inlet behind Black Point often has *Slavonian Grebe*. *Little Egrets* occur at low tide and large numbers of *Bar-tailed Godwit* gather north of the sailing club.
Access: The road onto the point is privately owned but access is only restricted during the summer months. Please park sensibly as vehicular access is permissive only. Alternatively, there is a public footpath along the Black Point peninsular which starts in Bracklesham Rd.

February

The Kench Local Nature Reserve (see page 28)
Timing: Low tide for feeding waders, high tide for wildfowl and roosting waders.
Species: Impressive numbers of *Redshank, Knot, Bar-tailed Godwit, Grey Plover* and *Turnstone* roost at the Local Nature Reserve at the Kench. Birds gather on the shingle bars as the tide rises. At high tide this can be a good place for close-up views of *Brent Geese, Goldeneye* and *Red-breasted Merganser*.
Access: The nearest car parks to the Kench are at Sinah Gravel Pit SZ 699 995 and at the end of Ferry Road SZ 688 998. Both are Havant BC pay and display car parks.

North Common, Northney (see page 26)
Timing: Rising/high tide.
Species: On a rising tide the saltmarsh south of Northney Marina often holds large flocks of *Golden Plover* and *Lapwing*. At high tide the old boating lake has a roost of *Redshank* and sometimes good sized flocks of *Teal*. The large grass field immediately to the south often contains *Brent Geese* and *Curlew*.
Access: Park in the Havant BC car park at SU 738 037 and walk out to the harbour along the footpath.

March

Sandy Point Nature Reserve (see page 55)
Timing: Last two weeks of March, mid-morning is often good.
Species: Look out for early returning migrants such as *Wheatears* on the fence line and open heathland. By the end of the month *Sandwich Terns* can be seen offshore.
Access: There is a footpath from Seafarers Walk at SZ 748 985 which leads out onto the seafront. From here you can walk along the beach and gain good views into the nature reserve

Sinah Gravel Pit area (see page 74)
Timing: Morning visits are usually best.
Species: Early returning migrant *Sand Martins* can be seen over the gravel pit and *Chiffchaffs* in the surrounding Sallows. *Dartford Warbler* in the gorse scrub.
Access: Havant BC car park next to the gravel pit at SZ 699 995. *No access to gravel pit.*

April

Sandy Point Nature Reserve (see page 71)
Timing: Guided walks usually start at 10.00am.
Species: Spring migrants including *Whitethroat, Lesser Whitethroat* and *Whinchat.* A good chance of resident *Dartford Warblers* and *Linnets.* Early flowering plants include *Spring Vetch* and *Early Dog Violet.* Butterflies may include *Speckled Wood* and *Holly Blue.*
Access: Parking for guided walks is by the first entrance gate to the nature reserve at the beginning of Seafarers Walk. SZ 746 984. Information on the Hampshire County Council Guided Walks programme is contained in a booklet available to buy, or from the Hayling library. Details are also carried in the local press, or you can call the Countryside Service office on 023 92 476411

Gunner Point (see page 39)
Timing: Last week of April.
Species: Thousands of *Green-winged Orchids* in flower with many other species in the rich turf behind Gunner Point beach. *Wheatears* and *Skylarks* can be seen on the vegetated shingle ridges.
Access: Park either at the Havant BC car park at the end of Ferry Road at SZ 688 998 or in the seafront car park at SZ 703 989 and walk round to Gunner Point.

Hayling Billy Coastal Path (see page 86)
Timing: Latter half of April on a low or rising tide.
Species: A walk along the Billy line should be colourful with flowering *Gorse* and *Blackthorn.* Birds include singing *Whitethroats* and *Yellowhammers.* *Whimbrel* and *Common Sandpiper* on passage occur in Langstone Harbour and can be seen from the coastal path.
Access: Park either at the Hayling Halt car park behind the Esso garage SU 717 029 and walk south down the line. Alternatively park in the car park next to the Station Theatre, Station Road SZ 709 998 and walk up the line.

May

Gunner Point (see page 40)
Timing: Not critical, just choose a nice day.
Species: Thousands of *Sea Kale* plants in full bloom along the shingle beach, also look out for the rare *Little Robin* which will be in flower by the end of the month. Many other species in the grassland behind the beach, including *Bird's-foot-trefoil* and *Yellow-rattle.* In sunny weather *Common Blue* butterflies often abundant.
Access: See details for April.

Hayling Billy Coastal Path (see page 86)
Timing: Not critical.
Species: The borrow pit in Saltmarsh Copse has breeding *Moorhen* and sometimes *Sedge Warbler.* This is also a good site for *Orange-tip* butterflies. Further up the line listen for calling *Turtle Doves* in the thick *Blackthorn* hedges around the West Lane fields.
Access: See details for April.

Sandy Point Seafront (see page 16)

Timing: Early morning, during the first two weeks of May. Best conditions are when the wind is from the east or south-east. A telescope is very useful when 'seawatching'.

Species: Migrating seabirds including *Auks, Divers, Terns* and *Skuas*. This is the best time of year to see species like *Gannet* and *Fulmar* which are normally scarce off Hayling.

Access: Park at the eastern end of Southwood Road and walk out onto the beach.

June

Hayling Oysterbeds and the Billy Line (see page 16)

Timing: Not critical.

Species: Little Terns can easily be observed fishing within the Oysterbeds Lagoon. Several pairs breed on the island within the lagoon. This the easiest place on Hayling to see this rare and attractive seabird. The coastal path next to the Oysterbeds has *Yellow-wort* and *Bee Orchid.*

Access: Park either at Hayling Halt SU 717 029 or at the top of the line at SU 719 039

Gunner Point (see page 16)

Timing: Not critical.

Species: Viper's-bugloss and the introduced *Tree Lupin* and *Rose Campion* turn Gunner Point into a colourful spectacle. *Yellow-horned Poppies* and *Little-robin* on the shingle beach. Watch for *Sandwich* and *Common Terns* flying out of Langstone Harbour to feed offshore. *Mediterranean Gulls* in summer plumage can also be seen around the harbour entrance.

Access: See details for April.

Beachlands (see page 16)

Timing: Not critical.

Species: Much of Beachlands is rich in wild plants. The vegetated shingle beach in front of the pitch and putt course has an impressive display of *Sea Pink (Thrift)*, also *Hare's-foot Clover, Suffocated Clover* and *Mossy Stonecrop.*

Access: Park in the beach car park at SZ 703 989.

July

Sandy Point Nature Reserve (see page 16)

Timing: For information about guided walks see details for April.

Species: Sand dune plants like *Sea Holly, Sea Bindweed* and *Sea Spurge* are now in flower. *Bell Heather* is in bloom on the maritime heath within the reserve. *Grayling* and *Small Copper* butterflies are very active on sunny days. *Grey Bush-crickets* can be found in the long grass on the dunes.

Access: Many of the sand dune plants can be seen while walking around the perimeter of the reserve. To see the variety of heathland wildlife within Sandy Point Nature Reserve, please join an organised guided walk.

The West Lane Fields (see page 16)

Timing: Not critical.

Species: Species-rich, ancient meadows with *Dyer's Greenweed, Corky-fruited Water-dropwort* and *Common Sorrel.* Butterflies include *Meadow Brown, Gatekeeper* and *Small Heath.*

Access: The two best fields lie next to the Coastal Path at approx SU 715 023. *Fields only accessible with the permission of the grazier,* but can easily be seen from the Coastal Path.

Northern section of the Hayling Billy Coastal Path (see page 90)
Timing: Not critical.
Species: The chalk banks here have abundant *Marjoram* and *Greater Knapweed* attracting *Marbled White* butterflies. The scarce *Spiny Restharrow* grows alongside the track with both *Common* and *Lesser Centaury*. By the end of the month *Great-green Bush-crickets* can be heard calling from the long vegetation.
Access: See details for June.

August
North Common, Northney (see page 67)
Timing: Not critical.
Species: The species-rich grassland contains *Strawberry Clover, Pepper-saxifrage* and *Slender Hare's-ear*. Migrant butterflies such as *Painted Lady* and *Clouded Yellow* often occur here. *Wasp Spiders* are common in the long grass. Migrant warblers gather in the scrub patches to feed on blackberries and elderberries.
Access: See details for February.

Gutner Point Local Nature Reserve (see page 20)
Timing: On a rising tide 2-3 hours before high tide.
Species: A spectacular roost of waders, many still in summer plumage with *Bar-tailed Godwit, Grey Plover, Dunlin, Curlew* and *Whimbrel*. Saltmarsh plants include flowering *Golden Samphire* and multi-coloured *Glassworts*. The *Oak* trees at Gutner contain a colony of *Purple Hairstreak* butterflies.
Access: Due to the risk of disturbing the large wader roost, access is restricted to organised groups led by HCC Countryside Service Rangers. For details please telephone: 023 92 476411.

September
The Kench Local Nature Reserve (see page 14)
Timing: Evening low tides.
Species: Large numbers of *Sandwich, Common* and *Little Terns* gather to roost on the old railway embankment north of the Kench.
Access: See details for February.
Note: A similar gathering of terns occurs on the 'shell island' to the west of Black Point.

Sandy Point Nature Reserve (see page 59)
Timing: For information about guided walks see details for April.
Species: Migrant birds and butterflies, flowering plants include *Evening-primrose* on the dunes. *Terns* and *Skuas* sometimes seen offshore.
Access: See details for April.

Northney Road Saltmarsh (see page 69)
Timing: Low tide for plants; rising tide for waders.
Species: A good range of saltmarsh plants including *Sea Aster* and *Golden Samphire*. On a rising tide, waders gathering on the marsh include *Black-tailed Godwit, Whimbrel* and *Redshank*. By mid-month the first *Brent Geese* have returned to the harbour.
Access: Park in the lay-by on Northney Road at SU 723 042 to view the area.

October

Ferry Road scrub and Sinah Gravel Pit

Timing: Mornings are usually best.

Species: Autumn migrants including *Goldcrests, Firecrests, warblers, pipits* and *finches.*

Access: Park next to the gravel pit at SZ 699 995 to access the areas of scrub alongside Ferry Road and the Sinah Warren Holiday Village. Large numbers of *Swallows* and *Martins* sometimes gather over the gravel pit.

Sandy Point (see page 59)

Timing: Mornings are usually best.

Species: Autumn migrants including *thrushes, warblers, Wheatears* and *Whinchats.*

Access: See details for March.

November

Sinah Gravel Pit (see page 74)

Timing: Not critical.

Species: The wintering flocks of *Tufted Duck, Pochard* and *Coot* can be seen along with *Little Grebe* and various species of *gull.*

Access: See details for March.

Hayling Billy Coastal Path (see page 23)

Timing: Rising tide for *waders*; high tide for *wildfowl* and *grebes.*

Species: *Oystercatchers* feed on the cockle beds; *Turnstone, Redshank* and *Rock Pipit* along the strandline; *Dunlin, Curlew* and *Grey Plover* on the mudflats. At high tide *Brent Geese* and *Great-crested Grebes* come close inshore.

Access: See details for April.

December

Black Point (see page 26)

Timing: Rising tide to high tide.

Species: *Sanderling* and *Ringed Plover* on the sandy beach north of Black Point. At high tide *Knot, Dunlin* and *Bar-tailed Godwit* join them to roost on the 'shell island' just west of the point.

Access: See details for January.

Gunner Point and The Kench (see page 16)

Timing: High tide at The Kench.

Species: A circular walk can reveal a range of *waders* and *wildfowl* at the Kench, followed by Sinah Gravel Pit to view waterbirds and Gunner Point beach for *finches* and *larks.*

Access: See details for April.

Species Lists

The following are lists of species which have been recorded on or from Hayling Island. These lists are in no way an exhaustive record of all Hayling's flora and as new species continue to be found while others become extinct.

We hope they provide a reasonable indication of the richness of Hayling Island's flora and fauna at the beginning of the new millennium.

Plants
The list of vascular plants includes all British native species recorded on Hayling Island as well as long established introduced and alien species. Some of the more scarce garden escapes and casuals have been omitted due to lack of space. The status given refers to the species status in Hampshire. We are grateful for the endeavours of Botanical Society of the British Isles (BSBI) members, without which this list would be far less complete.

Birds
The list includes all species of bird seen on, or observed from Hayling Island. It includes introduced and feral species which have self-sustaining populations in the UK. The status given refers to the species status on Hayling Island.

Mammal, reptiles and amphibians
Most mammals are nocturnal and notoriously difficult to survey. There is little information available on Hayling's bats and small mammals so despite the relatively few species involved this is perhaps the least complete list included.

Butterflies and moths
The list includes all species of larger 'macro' moth and butterfly known to have been recorded on Hayling Island. The list includes records provided by a number of resident and visiting entomologists.

Bullfinch

List of Bird Species recorded on or from Hayling Island

W-Winter   Sp-Spring   S-Summer
A-Autumn   * - breeds on Hayling

Species	Time of year
Red-throated Diver	Sp, A, W
Black-throated Diver	Sp, A, W
Great Northern Diver	Sp, A, W
Great Crested Grebe	All year
Red-necked Grebe	Sp, A, W
Little Grebe*	All year
Black-necked Grebe	Sp, A, W
Slavonian Grebe	Sp, A, W
Fulmar	Rare All year
Manx Shearwater	Rare, Sp, A
Mediterranean Shearwater	Rare Sp
Leach's Petrel	Rare, A, W
Gannet	Rare All year
Cormorant	All year
Shag	A, W
Bittern	Rare, W
Little Egret	All year
Great White Egret	Very rare (1985)
Grey Heron*	All year
Purple Heron	Very rare
White Stork	Very rare
Spoonbill	Rare, Sp, A
Mute Swan*	All year
Bewick's Swan	Rare, W
Bean Goose	Very rare, W
Pink-footed Goose	Very rare, W
White-fronted Goose	Rare, W
Greylag Goose	All year
Canada Goose*	All year
Barnacle Goose	Very rare, W
Brent Goose	Sp, A, W
Red-breasted Goose	Very Rare, W
Egyptian Goose	Escape - All year
Ruddy Shelduck	Escape - All year
Shelduck*	All year
Wigeon	Sp, A, W
Gadwall	Sp, A, W
Teal	Sp, A, W
Mallard*	All year
Pintail	Sp, A, W
Gargancy	Rare, Sp
Shoveler	Sp, A, W
Red-crested Pochard	Very Rare, W
Pochard	Sp, A, W
Tufted Duck*	All year
Scaup	Rare, W
Eider	Sp, A, W
Long-tailed Duck	Scarce, Sp, A, W
Common Scoter	Sp, A, W
Velvet Scoter	Scarce, Sp, A, W

Goldeneye	Sp, A, W
Smew	Scarce, W
Red-breasted Merganser	Sp, A, W
Goosander	Scarce, W
Ruddy Duck	Scarce, W
Honey Buzzard	Rare, Sp, A
Black Kite	Very rare, Sp
Marsh Harrier	Scarce, Sp, A
Hen Harrier	Scarce, W
Montagu's Harrier	Very Rare, A
Sparrowhawk*	All year
Buzzard	Scarce, Sp, A, W
Osprey	Scarce, Sp, A
Kestrel*	All year
Red-footed Falcon	Very rare, (1997)
Merlin	Sp, A, W
Hobby	Sp, S, A
Peregrine	W
Red-legged Partridge*	All year
Grey Partridge*	All year
Quail	Rare, Sp, S
Pheasant*	All year
Water Rail	Sp, A, W
Corncrake	Very rare, A
Moorhen*	All year
Coot*	All year
Crane	Very rare, A
Oystercatcher*	All year
Black-winged Stilt	Very rare, Sp
Avocet	Rare, W
Stone-curlew	Rare, Sp, A
Little Ringed Plover	Rare, Sp, A
Ringed Plover*	All year
Kentish Plover	Very Rare, Sp, W
Dotterel	Very rare, Sp
Golden Plover	Sp, A, W
Grey Plover	All year
Lapwing*	All year
Knot	Sp, A, W

Avocet

115

Sanderling	Sp, A, W
Little Stint	Scarce, Sp, A, W
Temminck's Stint	Rare, Sp, A
Baird's Sandpiper	Very rare, A (2000)
Curlew Sandpiper	Scarce, Sp, A
Purple Sandpiper	Scarce, W
Dunlin	All year
Buff-breasted Sandpiper	Very rare, A (1983)
Ruff	Scarce, W
Jack Snipe	Scarce, A, W
Common Snipe	A, W
Woodcock	A, W
Black-tailed Godwit	All year
Bar-tailed Godwit	All year
Whimbrel	Sp, S, A
Curlew	All year
Spotted Redshank	Sp, A, W
Redshank*	All year
Greenshank	All year
Green Sandpiper	A, W
Wood Sandpiper	Scarce, A
Common Sandpiper	Sp, A
Turnstone	All year
Grey Phalarope	Scarce, A, W
Pomarine Skua	Scarce, Sp, A
Arctic Skua	Sp, A
Long-tailed Skua	Very rare, Sp (1986)
Great Skua	Scarce, Sp, A
Mediterranean Gull*	All year
Little Gull	Sp, A, W
Sabine's Gull	Rare, A, W
Black-headed Gull*	All year
Ring-billed Gull	Rare, W
Common Gull	Sp, A, W
Lesser Black-backed Gull	Sp, A, W
Herring Gull	All year
Iceland Gull	Rare, W
Glaucous Gull	Scarce, W
Great Black-backed Gull	All year
Kittiwake	Sp, A, W
Gull-billed Tern	Very rare (1958)
Sandwich Tern*	Sp, S, A
Roseate Tern	Scarce, Sp, A
Common Tern*	Sp, S, A
Arctic Tern	Scarce, Sp, A
Little Tern*	Sp, S, A
Black Tern	Sp, A
White-winged Black Tern	Very Rare, Sp, A
Guillemot	W
Razorbill	W
Little Auk	Rare, W
Puffin	Rare, Sp
Pallas's Sandgrouse	Very rare (12 in 1888)
Feral Pigeon*	All year
Stock Dove*	All year
Woodpigeon*	All year
Collared Dove*	All year
Turtle Dove*	Sp, S, A

Meadow Pipit

Ring-necked Parakeet	Scarce, all year
Cuckoo*	Sp, S, A
Barn Owl*	All year
Little Owl*	All year
Tawny Owl*	All year
Long-eared Owl	Scarce, W
Short-eared Owl	Scarce, W
Nightjar	Rare, Sp, A
Swift*	Sp, S
Kingfisher	A, W
Bee-eater	Very rare (2000)
Hoopoe	Rare, Sp, A
Wryneck	Rare, Sp, A
Green Woodpecker*	All year
Great Spotted Woodpecker*	All year
Lesser Spotted Woodpecker	Scarce, A, W
Woodlark	Rare, A, W
Skylark*	All year
Shore Lark	Rare, W
Sand Martin	Sp, S, A
Swallow*	Sp, S, A
House Martin*	Sp, S, A
Tawny Pipit	Very rare (1982)
Tree Pipit	Sp, A
Meadow Pipit*	All year
Rock Pipit	A, W
Water Pipit	Scarce, W
Yellow Wagtail	Sp, A
Grey Wagtail	Sp, A, W
Pied Wagtail*	All year
Wren*	All year
Dunnock*	All year
Robin*	All year
Nightingale*	Sp, S, A
Bluethroat	Very rare (1996)
Black Redstart	Scarce, W
Redstart	Sp, A
Whinchat	Sp, A
Stonechat*	All year
Wheatear	Sp, S, A
Ring Ouzel	Scarce, Sp, A
Blackbird*	All year
Fieldfare	A, W

Song Thrush*	All year	Nuthatch	Rare
Redwing	A, W	Treecreeper*	All year
Mistle Thrush*	All year	Golden Oriole	Rare, Sp
Cetti's Warbler	Scarce, W	Red-backed Shrike	Rare, A
Grasshopper Warbler	Sp, A	Jay*	All year
Aquatic Warbler	Very rare, A	Magpie*	All year
Sedge Warbler*	Sp, S, A	Jackdaw*	All year
Marsh Warbler	Very rare, Sp	Rook*	All year
Reed Warbler*	Sp, S, A	Carrion Crow*	All year
Icterine Warbler	Very rare, A (1992)	Raven	Rare
Melodious Warbler	Very rare, (1983)	Starling*	All year
Dartford Warbler*	All year	House Sparrow*	All year
Subalpine Warbler	Very rare (1984)	Tree Sparrow	Rare, A, W
Lesser Whitethroat*	Sp, S, A	Chaffinch*	All year
Whitethroat*	Sp, S, A	Brambling	Scarce, A, W
Garden Warbler	Sp, A	Greenfinch*	All year
Blackcap*	All year	Goldfinch*	All year
Yellow-browed Warbler	Rare, A	Siskin	A,W
Wood Warbler	Sp, A	Serin	Very rare (2000)
Chiffchaff*	All year	Linnet*	All year
Willow Warbler*	Sp, S, A	Twite	Rare, W
Goldcrest*	All year	Redpoll	A, W
Firecrest	A,W	Crossbill	Scarce, S, A,W
Spotted Flycatcher*	Sp, S, A	Bullfinch*	All year
Red-breasted Flycatcher	Very rare (1989)	Lapland Bunting	Rare, A,W
Pied Flycatcher	Sp, A	Snow Bunting	Scarce, A,W
Bearded Tit	Rare, A	Yellowhammer*	All year
Long-tailed Tit*	All year	Cirl Bunting	Very Rare, W, last bred in 1968
Marsh Tit	Scarce, W	Ortolan Bunting	Very Rare, A (1984)
Coal Tit*	All year	Reed Bunting*	All year
Blue Tit*	All year	Corn Bunting	Rare, W, last bred in 1980s
Great Tit*	All year		

Little Egret and Redshanks

117

Odonata (Dragonflies and Damselflies)

Large Red Damselfly — *Pyrrhosoma nymphula*
Common Blue Damselfly — *Enallagma cyathigerum*
Azure Damselfly — *Coenagrion puella*
Blue-tailed Damselfly — *Ischnura elegans*
Southern Hawker — *Aeshna cyanea*
Migrant Hawker — *Aeshna mixta*
Emperor Dragonfly — *Anax imperator*
Downy Emerald — *Cordulia aenea*
Four-spotted Chaser — *Libellula quadrimaculata*
Broad-bodied Chaser — *Libellula depressa*
Black-tailed Skimmer — *Libellula cancellatum*
Common Darter — *Sympetrum striolatum*
Ruddy Darter — *Sympetrum sanguineum*

Migrant Hawker

Orthoptera (Grasshoppers, crickets and allied insects)

Oak Bush-cricket — *Meconema thalassinum*
Great Green Bush-cricket — *Tettigonia viridissima*
Dark Bush-cricket — *Pholidoptera griseoaptera*
Grey Bush-cricket — *Platycleis albopunctata*
Long-winged Cone-head — *Conocephalus discolor*
Short-winged Cone-head — *Conocephalus dorsalis*
Speckled Bush-cricket — *Leptophyes punctatissima*
Common Ground-hopper — *Tetrix undulata*
Woodland Grasshopper — *Omocestus rufipes*
Field Grasshopper — *Chorthippus brunneus*
Meadow Grasshopper — *Chorthippus parallelus*
Lesser Marsh Grasshopper — *Chorthippus albomarginatus*
Mottled Grasshopper — *Myrmeleotettix maculatus*
Lesser Cockroach — *Ectobius panzeri*
Common Earwig — *Forficula auricularia*

Long-winged Cone-head

Bumble bees

Common White-tailed Bumble bee	*Bombus lucorum*	common
Buff-tailed Bumble bee	*Bombus terrestris*	common
a Bumble bee	*Bombus cullumanus*	1 in 1919, now extinct in UK
Small Heath Bumble bee	*Bombus jonellus*	scarce (Sinah and Sandy Point)
Meadow Bumble bee	*Bombus pratorum*	common
Large Red-tailed Bumble bee	*Bombus lapidarius*	common
Garden Bumble bee	*Bombus hortorum*	common
Moss Carder bee	*Bombus muscorum*	rare (Sinah and Sandy Point)
Common Carder bee	*Bombus pascuorum*	common
Small Red-tailed Bumble bee	*Bombus ruderarius*	rare (Sinah)
Short-haired Bumble bee	*Bombus subterraneus*	last seen 1883, now extinct in UK
Vestal Cuckoo bee	*Bombus vestalis*	common

White-tailed Bumble bee

Mammals

Common Seal	*Phoca vitulinus*
Grey Seal	*Halichoerus grypus*
Mole	*Talpa europaea*
Common Shrew	*Sorex araneus*
Hedgehog	*Erinaceus europaeus*
Pipistrelle Bat	*Pipistrellus pipistrellus*
Fox	*Vulpes vulpes*
Weasel	*Mustela nivalis*
Rabbit	*Oryctolagus cuniculus*
Brown Hare	*Lepus capensis*
Grey Squirrel	*Sciurus carolinensis*
Short-tailed Vole	*Microtus agrestis*
Wood or	
Long-tailed Fieldmouse	*Apodemus sylvaticus*
Harvest Mouse	*Micromys minutus*
Brown Rat	*Rattus norvegicus*
House Mouse	*Mus musculus*
Roe Deer	*Capreolus capreolus*
Harbour Porpoise	*Phocoena phocoena*

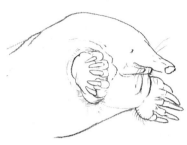

Mole

Reptiles

Slow-worm	*Anguis fragilis*
Common Lizard	*Lacerta vivapara*
Grass Snake	*Natrix natrix*
Adder	*Vipera berus*

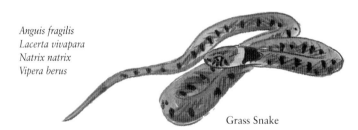

Grass Snake

Amphibians

Smooth Newt	*Triturus vulgaris*
Great Crested Newt	*Triturus cristatus*
Palmate Newt	*Triturus helveticus*
Common Frog	*Rana temporaria*
Common Toad	*Bufo bufo*

Common Toad

Lepidoptera (Butterflies and moths)

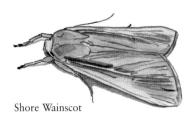

Shore Wainscot

Moths

Ghost Moth *Hepialus humuli*
Orange Swift *Hepialus sylvina*
Gold Swift *Hepialus hecta*
Common Swift *Hepialus lupulinus*
Leopard Moth *Zeuzera pyrina*
Goat Moth *Cossus cossus*
Six Spot Burnet *Zygaena filipendulae*
Narrow-bordered Five Spot Burnet *Zygaena lonicerae*
Lunar Hornet *Sesia bembeciformis*
Currant Clearwing *Synanthedon tipuliformis*
Fiery Clearwing *Bembecia chrysidiformis* (Extinct)
December Moth *Poecilocampa populi*
Lackey *Malacosoma neustria*
Grass Eggar *Lasiocampa trifolii*
Oak Eggar *Lasiocampa quercus*
Fox Moth *Macrothylacia rubi*
Drinker *Euthrix potatoria*
Emperor *Saturnia pavonia*
Scalloped Hook Tip *Falcaria lacertinaria*
Oak Hook Tip *Watsonalla binaria*
Pebble Hook Tip *Drepana falcataria*
Chinese Character *Cilix glaucata*
Peach Blossom *Thyatira batis*
Buff Arches *Habrosyne pyritoides*
Figure Of Eighty *Tethea ocularis*
Common Lutestring *Ochropacha duplaris*
March Moth *Alsophila aescularia*
Grass Emerald *Pseudoterpna pruinata*
Large Emerald *Geometra papilionaria*
Blotched Emerald *Comibaena bajularia*
Common Emerald *Hemithea aestivaria*
Little Emerald *Jodis lactearia*
The Mocha *Cyclophora annularia*
Maidens Blush *Cyclophora punctaria*
Blood Vein *Timandra comae*
Mullien Wave *Scopula marginepunctata*
Small Blood-vein *Scopula imitaria*
Rosy Wave *Scopula emutaria*
Cream Wave *Scopula floslactata*
Least Carpet *Idaea rusticata atrosignaria*
Small Fan-footed Wave *Idaea biselata*
Dwarf-Cream Wave *Idaea fuscovenosa*
Small-Dusty Wave *Idaea seriata*
Single-Dotted Wave *Idaea dimidiata*
Satin Wave *Idaea subsericeata*
Treble Brown-Spot *Idaea trigeminata*
Small Scallop *Idaea emarginata*
Riband Wave *Idaea aversata*
The Vestal *Rhodometra sacraria*

Oblique Striped *Phibalapteryx virgata*
The Gem *Orthonama obstipata*
Flame Carpet *Xanthorhoe designata*
Red Twin-spot Carpet *Xanthorhoe spadicearia*
Dark-barred Twin-spot Carpet *Xanthorhoe ferrugata*
Silver-ground Carpet *Xanthorhoe montanata*
Garden Carpet *Xanthorhoe fluctuata*
Shaded Broad-bar *Scotopteryx chenopodiata*
Ruddy Carpet *Catarhoe rubidata*
Royal Mantle *Catarhoe cuculata*
Common Carpet *Epirrhoe alternata*
Wood Carpet *Epirrhoe rivata*
Galium Carpet *Epirrhoe galiata*
Yellow Shell *Camptogramma bilineata*
The Mallow *Larentia clavaria*
Shoulder Stripe *Anticlea badiata*
The Streamer *Anticlea derivata*
Water Carpet *Lampropteryx suffumata*
Purple Bar *Cosmorhoe ocellata*
The Pheonix *Eulithis prunata*
The Spinach *Eulithis mellinata*
Barred Straw *Eulithis pyraliata*
Small Pheonix *Ecliptopera silaceata*
Common Marbled Carpet *Chloroclysta truncata*
Barred Yellow *Cidaria fulvata*
Blue-bordered Carpet *Plemyria rubiginata*
Pine Carpet *Thera firmata*
Grey Pine Carpet *Thera obeliscata*
Spruce Carpet *Thera britannica*
Cypress Carpet *Thera cupressata*
Broken-barred Carpet *Electrophaes corylata*
Mottled Grey *Colostygia multistrigaria*
Green Carpet *Colostygia pectinataria*
May Highflyer *Hydriomena impluviata*
July Highflyer *Hydriomena furcata*
Small Waved Umber *Horisme vitalbata*
Pretty Chalk Carpet *Melanthia procellata*
Scallop Shell *Rheumaptera undulata*
Sharp Angled Carpet *Euphyia unangulata*
November Moth *Epirrita dilutata*
Winter Moth *Operophtera brumata*
Small Rivulet *Perizoma alchemillata*
Barred Rivulet *Perizoma bifaciata*
Slender Pug *Eupithecia tenuiata*
Haworth's Pug *Eupithecia haworthiata*
Toadflax Pug *Eupithecia linariata*
Foxglove Pug *Eupithecia pulchellata*
Pinion-spotted Pug *Eupithecia insigniata*
Mottled Pug *Eupithecia exiguata*
Lime-speck Pug *Eupithecia centaureata*
Freyer's Pug *Eupithecia intricata*
Wormwood Pug *Eupithecia absinthiata*
Currant Pug *Eupithecia assimilata*
Bleached Pug *Eupithecia expallidata*
Common Pug *Eupithecia vulgata*
White-spotted Pug *Eupithecia tripunctaria*
Grey Pug *Eupithecia subfuscata*
Tawny-speckled Pug *Eupithecia icterata*
Bordered Pug *Eupithecia succenturiata*
Shaded Pug *Eupithecia subumbrata*
Yarrow Pug *Eupithecia millefoliata*
Plain Pug *Eupithecia simpliciata*
Ochreous Pug *Eupithecia indigata* .
Narrow-winged Pug *Eupithecia nanata*

Brindled Pug *Eupithecia abbreviata*
Oak-tree Pug *Eupithecia dodoneata*
Cypress Pug *Eupithecia phoeniceata*
Channel Islands Pug *Eupithecia ultimaria*
V-Pug *Chloroclystis v-ata*
Green Pug *Chloroclystis rectangulata*
Double-striped Pug *Gymnoscelis rufifasciata*
The Streak *Chesias legatella*
Treble-bar *Aplocera plagiata*
Lesser Treble-bar *Aplocera efformata*
Small White Wave *Asthena albulata*
Small Yellow Wave *Hydrelia flammeolaria*
The Seraphim *Lobophora halterata*
Early Tooth-striped *Trichopteryx carpinata*
Small Seraphim *Pterapherapteryx sexalata*
Yellow-barred Brindle *Acasis viretata*
The Magpie *Abraxas grossulariata*
Clouded Border *Lomaspilis marginata*
Scorched Carpet *Ligdia adustata*
Peacock *Macaria notata*
Sharp-angled Peacock *Macaria alternata*
Tawny-barred Angle *Macaria liturata*
Brown Silver-line *Petrophora chlorosata*
Barred Umber *Plagodis pulveraria*
Scorched Wing *Plagodis dolabraria*
Brimstone Moth *Opisthograptis luteolata*
Bordered Beauty *Epione repandaria*
Speckled Yellow *Pseudopanthera macularia*
Lilac Beauty *Apeira syringaria*
Large Thorn *Ennomos autumnaria*
August Thorn *Ennomos quercinaria*
Canary-shouldered Thorn *Ennomos alniaria*
Dusky Thorn *Ennomos fuscantaria*
September Thorn *Ennomos erosaria*
Early Thorn *Selenia dentaria*
Purple Thorn *Selenia tetralunaria*
Scalloped Hazel *Odontopera bidentata*
Scalloped Oak *Crocallis elinguaria*
Swallow-tailed Moth *Ourapteryx sambucaria*
Feathered Thorn *Colotois pennaria*
Small Brindled Beauty *Apocheima hispidaria*
Pale Brindled Beauty *Apocheima pilosaria*
Brindled Beauty *Lycia hirtaria*
Oak Beauty *Biston strataria*
Peppered Moth *Biston betularia*
Spring Usher *Agriopis leucophaearia*
Dotted Border *Agriopis marginaria*
Mottled Umber *Erannis defoliaria*
Waved Umber *Menophora abruptaria*
Willow Beauty *Peribatodes rhomboidaria*
Bordered Grey *Selidosema brunnearia*
Mottled Beauty *Alcis repandata repandata*
The Engrailed *Ectropis bistortata*
Small Engrailed *Ectropis crepuscularia*
Grey Birch *Aethalura punctulata*
Common Heath *Ematurga atomaria*
Bordered White *Bupalis piniaria*
Common White Wave *Cabera pusaria*
Common Wave *Cabera exanthemata*
White-pinion Spotted *Lomographa bimaculata*
Clouded Silver *Lomographa temerata*
Early Moth *Theria primaria*
Light Emerald *Campaea margaritata*
Barred Red *Hylaea fasciaria*
Yellow Belle *Semiaspilates ochrearia*

Convolvulus Hawk-moth *Agrius convolvuli*
Deaths-head Hawk-moth *Acherontia atropos*
Privet Hawk-moth *Sphinx ligustri*
Pine Hawk-moth *Hyloicus pinastri*
Lime Hawk-moth *Mimas tiliae*
Eyed Hawk-moth *Smerinthus ocellata*
Poplar Hawk-moth *Laothoe populi*
Humming-bird Hawk-moth *Macroglossum stellatarum*
Elephant Hawk-moth *Deilephila elpenor*
Small Elephant Hawk-moth *Deilephila porcellus*
Puss Moth *Cerura vinula*
Sallow Kitten *Furcula furcula*
Poplar Kitten *Furcula bifida*
Iron Prominent *Notodonta dromedarius*
Pebble Prominent *Notodonta ziczac*
Lesser Swallow Prominent *Pheosia gnoma*
Swallow Prominent *Pheosia tremula*
Coxcomb Prominent *Ptilodon capucina*
Pale Prominent *Pterostoma palpina*
Marbled Brown *Drymonia dodonaea*
Lunar Marbled Brown *Drymonia ruficornis*
Chocolate-tip *Clostera curtula*
Buff-tip *Phalera bucephala*
Lobster Moth *Stauropus fagi*
Figure of Eight *Diloba caeruleocephala*
The Vapourer *Orgyia antiqua*
Pale Tussock *Calliteara pudibunda*
Brown-tail *Euproctis chrysorrhoea*
Yellow-tail *Euproctis similis*
White Satin *Leucoma salicis*
Black Arches *Lymantria monacha*
Rosy Footman *Miltochrista miniata*
Four-dotted Footman *Cybosia mesomella*
Orange Footman *Eilema sororcula*
Dingy Footman *Eilema griseola*
Scarce Footman *Eilema complana*
Buff Footman *Eilema depressa*
Common Footman *Eilema lurideola*
Crimson Speckled *Utetheisa pulchella*
Garden Tiger *Arctia caja*
Cream-spot Tiger *Arctia villica*
White Ermine *Spilosoma lubricipeda*
Buff Ermine *Spilosoma luteum*
Muslin Moth *Diaphora mendica*
Ruby Tiger *Phragmatobia fuliginosa*
Cinnabar *Tyria jacobaeae*
Kent Black Arches *Meganola albula*
Short-cloaked Moth *Nola cucullatella*
Least Black Arches *Nola confusalis*
White Line Dart *Euxoa tritici*
Garden Dart *Euxoa nigricans*
Archer's Dart *Agrotis vestigialis*
Turnip Moth *Agrotis segetum*
Heart & Club *Agrotis clavis*
Heart & Dart *Agrotis exclamationis*
Dark Sword-grass *Agrotis ipsilon*
Shuttle-shaped Dart *Agrotis puta*
Sand Dart *Agrotis ripae* Hb.
The Flame *Axylia putris* Linn.
Flame Shoulder *Ochropleura plecta* Linn.
Dotted Rustic *Rhyacia simulans* Hufn.
Large Yellow Underwing *Noctua pronuba*
Lesser Yellow Underwing *Noctua comes*
Broad Bordered Yellow Underwing *Noctua fimbriata*
Lesser Broad Bordered Yellow Underwing *Noctua janthe*

Least Yellow Underwing *Noctua interjecta*
True-lovers Knot *Lycophotia porphyrea*
Pearly Underwing *Peridroma saucia*
Ingrailed Clay *Diarsia mendica mendica*
Small Square Spot *Diarsia rubi*
Setaceous Hebrew Character *Xestia c-nigrum*
Double Square Spot *Xestia triangulum*
Dotted Clay *Xestia baja*
Six-striped Rustic *Xestia sexstrigata*
Square-spot Rustic *Xestia xanthographa*
Heath Rustic *Xestia agathina agathina*
The Gothic *Naenia typica* Linn.
Green Arches *Anaplectoides prasina* D.& S.
Beautiful Yellow Underwing *Anarta myrtilli*
The Nutmeg *Discestra trifolli*
The Shears *Hada plebeja*
Silvery Arches *Polia trimaculosa*
Grey Arches *Polia nebulosa*
White Colon *Sideridis albicolon*
Cabbage Moth *Mamestra brassicae*
Dot Moth *Melanchra persicariae*
Broom Moth *Melanchra pisi*
Light Brocade *Lacanobia w-latinum*
Pale-shouldered Brocade *Lacanobia thalassina*
Dog's Tooth *Lacanobia suasa*
Bright-line Brown-eye *Lacanobia oleracea*
Broad-barred White *Aetheria bicolorata*
The Campion *Hadena rivularis*
Tawny Shears *Hadena perplexa perplexa*
Varied Coronet *Hadena compta*
Marbled Coronet *Hadena confusa*
The Lychnis *Hadena bicruris*
Antler Moth *Cerapteryx graminis*
Hedge Rustic *Tholera cespitis*
Feathered Gothic *Tholera decimalis*
Pine Beauty *Panolis flammea*
Small Quaker *Orthosia cruda*
Blossom Underwing *Orthosia miniosa*
Powdered Quaker *Orthosia gracilis*
Common Quaker *Orthosia cerasi*
Clouded Drab *Orthosia incerta*
Twin-spot Quaker *Orthosia munda*
Hebrew Character *Orthosia gothica*
Brown-line Bright-eye *Mythimna conigera*
The Clay *Mythimna ferrago*
White Point *Mythimna albipuncta*
The Delicate *Mythimna vitellina*
Striped Wainscot *Mythimna pudorina*
SouthernWainscot *Mythimna straminea*
Smoky Wainscot *Mythimna impura impura*
Common Wainscot *Mythimna pallens*
Mathew's Wainscot *Mythimna favicolor*
Shore Wainscot *Mythimna litoralis*
L-album Wainscot *Mythimna l-album*
White-speck Wainscot *Mythimna unipuncta*
Shoulder Striped Wainscot *Mythimna comma*
The Cosmopolitan *Mythimna loreyi*
The Wormwood *Cucullia absinthii*
Chamomile Shark *Cucullia chamomillae*
The Shark *Cucullia umbratica*
The Mullein *Cucullia verbasci*
Star-wort *Cucullia asteris*
Minor Shoulder-knot *Brachylomia viminalis*
Deep-brown Dart *Aporophyla lutulenta*
Black Rustic *Aporophyla nigra*

Tawny Pinion *Lithophane semibrunnea*
Pale Pinion *Lithophane hepatica*
Grey Shoulder-knot *Lithophane ornitopus*
Blair's Shoulder-knot *Lithophane leautieri*
Early Grey *Xylocampa areola*
Green-brindled Crescent *Allophyes oxyacanthae*
Merveille du-jour *Dichonia aprilina*
Brindled Green *Dryobotodes eremita*
Flame Brocade *Trigonophora flammea*
Large Ranunculus *Polymixis flavicincta*
Feathered Ranunculus *Polymixis lichenea*
The Satellite *Eupsilia transversa*
The Chestnut *Conistra vaccinii*
The Brick *Agrochola circellaris*
Red-line Quaker *Agrochola lota*
Yellow-line Quaker *Agrochola macilenta*
Beaded Chestnut *Agrochola lychnidis*
Centre-barred Sallow *Atethmia centrago*
Lunar Underwing *Omphaloscelis lunosa*
Orange Sallow *Xanthia citrago*
Barred Sallow *Xanthia aurago*
Pink-barred Sallow *Xanthia togata*
The Sallow *Xanthia icteritia*
Dusky-lemon Sallow *Xanthia gilvago*
Poplar Grey *Acronicta megacephala*
The Sycamore *Acronicta aceris*
The Miller *Acronicta leporina*
Alder Dagger *Acronicta alni*
Dark Dagger *Acronicta tridens*
Grey Dagger *Acronicta psi*
Knot-grass *Acronicta rumicis*
The Coronet *Craniophora ligustri*
Marbled Beauty *Cryphia domestica*
Marbled Green *Cryphia muralis muralis*
Tree-lichen Beauty *Cryphia algae*
Copper Underwing *Amphipyra pyramidea*
Svensson's Copper Underwing *Amphipyra berbera*
Mouse Moth *Amphipyra tragopoginis*
Old Lady *Mormo maura*
Bird's Wing *Dypterygia scabriuscula*
Brown Rustic *Rusina ferruginea*
Straw Underwing *Thalpophila matura*
Small Angle Shades *Euplexia lucipara*
Angle Shades *Phlogophora meticulosa*
Double Kidney *Ipimorpha retusa*
The Olive *Ipimorpha subtusa*
Dingy Shears *Parastichtis ypsillon*
Dun- bar *Cosmia trapezina*
Lunar-spotted Pinion *Cosmia pyralina*
Dark Arches *Apamea monoglypha*
Light Arches *Apamea lithoxylaea*
Reddish Light Arches *Apamea sublustris*
Crescent Striped *Apamea oblonga*
Clouded Border Brindle *Apamea crenata*
Clouded Brindle *Apamea epomidion*
Dusky Brocade *Apamea remissa*
Small Clouded Brindle *Apamea unanimis*
Rustic Shoulder-knot *Apamea sordens*
Double Lobed *Apamea ophiogramma*
Marbled Minor *Oligia strigilis*
Tawny Marbled Minor *Oligia latruncula*
Middle-barred Minor *Oligia fasciuncula*
Cloaked Minor *Mesoligia furuncula*
Rosy Minor *Mesoligia literosa*
Common Rustic *Mesapamea secalis*

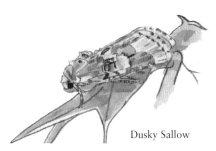

Dusky Sallow

Lesser Common Rustic *Mesapamea didyma*
Small Dotted Buff *Photedes minima*
Small Wainscot *Chortodes pygmina*
Dusky Sallow *Eremobia ochroleuca*
Flounced Rustic *Luperina testacea*
Saltern Ear *Amphipoea fucosa paludis*
Ear Moth *Amphipoea oculea*
Rosy Rustic *Hydraecia micacea*
Frosted Orange *Gortyna flavago*
The Crescent *Celaena leucostigma*
Bulrush Wainscot *Nonagria typhae*
Brown-veined Wainscot *Archanara dissoluta*
Large Wainscot *Rhizedra lutosa*
Fen Wainscot *Arenostola phragmitidis*
Treble Lines *Charanyca trigrammica*
The Uncertain *Hoplodrina alsines*
The Rustic *Hoplodrina blanda*
Vine's Rustic *Hoplodrina ambigua*
Small Mottled Willow *Spodoptera exigua*
Mottled Rustic *Caradrina morpheus*
Pale Mottled Willow *Paradrina clavipalpis*
Silky Wainscot *Chilodes maritimus*
Rosy Marbled *Elaphria venustula*
Small Yellow Underwing *Panemeria tenebrata*
Bordered Sallow *Pyrrhia umbra*
Scarce Bordered Straw *Helicoverpa armigera*
Bordered Straw *Heliothis peltigera*
Cream Bordered Green Pea *Earias clorana*
Scarce Silver-lines *Bena bicolorana*
Green Silver-lines *Pseudoips prasinana*
Oak Nycteoline *Nycteola revayana*
Nut Tree Tussock *Colocasia coryli*
The Ni Moth *Trichoplusia ni*
Burnished Brass *Diachrysia chrysitis*
Dewick's Plusia *Macdunnoughia confusa*
Golden Plusia *Polychrysia moneta*
Gold Spot *Plusia festucae*
Silver Y *Autographa gamma*
Beautiful Golden Y *Autographa pulchrina*
Plain Golden Y *Autographa jota*
Dark Spectacle *Abrostola triplasia*
The Spectacle *Abrostola tripartita*
Red Underwing *Catocala nupta*
Dark Crimson Underwing *Catocala sponsa*
Mother Shipton *Callistege mi*
The Blackneck *Lygephila pastinum*
The Herald *Scoliopteryx libatrix*
Small Purple-bar *Phytometra viridaria*
Beautiful Hook-tip *Laspeyria flexula*
Straw Dot *Rivula sericealis*
The Snout *Hypena proboscidalis*
Buttoned Snout *Hypena rostralis*
Pinion-streaked Snout *Schrankia costaestrigalis*
Small Fan-foot *Herminia grisealis*

Butterflies

European Swallowtail	vagrant from Europe (1945)
Small Skipper	resident
Essex Skipper	resident
Large Skipper	resident
Clouded Yellow	regular migrant
Brimstone	resident
Large White	resident and migrant
Small White	resident and migrant
Green-veined White	resident
Bath White	vagrant from Europe (1859 & 1945)
Orange-tip	resident
Purple Hairstreak	resident
Small Copper	resident
Long-tailed Blue	vagrant from Europe (1945)
Brown Argus	resident
Common Blue	resident
Chalkhill Blue	rare wanderer from chalk downs
Holly Blue	resident
White Admiral	resident
Red Admiral	resident and migrant
Painted Lady	common migrant
Small Tortoiseshell	resident
Large Tortoiseshell	extinct (last recorded in 1947)
Peacock	resident
Comma	resident
Pearl-bordered Fritillary	rare wanderer from mainland
Dark Green Fritillary	rare wanderer from mainland
Speckled Wood	resident
Wall	resident
Marbled White	resident
Grayling	resident
Gatekeeper	resident
Meadow Brown	resident
Small Heath	resident
Monarch	vagrant from America (1981)

Brimstone

123

Plants

Includes some well-established garden escapes, alien introductions and widespread plantings.

Frequency of occurence

VC= Very Common, C=Common, LC=Locally Common, F=Frequent, O= Occasional, L=Local, VL=Very Local, R=Rare, VR= Very Rare, E=Extinct

Status in Hampshire
(N)=Native, (A)=Alien, (C)= Casual, (E)=Established, (S)=Surviving, (P)=Planted

Species name	English name	Frequency	Status
Acer campestre	Field Maple	VC	(N)
Acer platanoides	Norway Maple	L	(C)
Acer pseudoplatanus	Sycamore	C	(E)
Achillea millefolium	Yarrow	C	(N)
Acorus calamus	Sweet Flag	R	(E)
Aegopodium podagraria	Ground Elder	VC	(E)
Aesculus hippocastanum	Horse Chestnut	C	(S)
Aethusa cynapium	Fool's Parsley	C	(N)
Agrimonia eupatoria	Common Agrimony	VC	(N)
Agrimonia procera	Fragrant Agrimony	L	(N)
Agrostis canina	Velvet Bent	LC	(N)
Agrostis capillaris	Fine Bent	F	(N)
Agrostis curtisii	Bristle Bent	LC	(N)
Agrostis gigantea	Black Bent	F	(N)
Agrostis stolonifera	Creeping Bent	F	(N)
Aira caryophyllea	Silver Hair-grass	L	(N)
Aira praecox	Early Hair-grass	LC	(N)
Ajuga reptans	Bugle	C	(N)
Alliaria petiolata	Garlic Mustard	VC	(N)
Allium triquetrum	Three-cornered Leek	VR	(C)
Allium vineale	Crow Garlic	F	(N)
Alnus glutinosa	Alder	LC	(N)
Alopecurus bulbosus	Bulbous Foxtail	VR	(N)
Alopecurus geniculatus	Marsh Foxtail	LC	(N)
Alopecurus myosuroides	Slender Foxtail	LC	(N)
Alopecurus pratensis	Meadow Foxtail	C	(N)
Ammophila arenaria	Marram Grass	L	(N)
Anacamptis pyramidalis	Pyramidal Orchid	L	(N)
Anagallis arvensis	Scarlet Pimpernel	VC	(N)
Anagallis arvensis ssp.	Blue Pimpernel	VR	(N)
Anchusa arvensis	Small Bugloss	LC	(E)
Anemone nemorosa	Wood Anemone	LC	(N)
Angelica sylvestris	Wild Angelica	LC	(N)
Anisantha rigida	Ripgut Brome	VR	(C)
Anisantha sterilis	Barren Brome	C	(N)
Anthemis tinctoria	Yellow Chamomile	L	(C)
Anthoxanthum odoratum	Sweet Vernal-grass	VC	(N)
Anthriscus caucalis	Bur Chervil	L	(N)
Anthriscus sylvestris	Cow Parsley	VC	(N)
Anthyllis vulneraria	Kidney Vetch	LC	(N)
Aphanes arvensis	Parsley-piert	C	(N)
Aphanes australis	Slender Parsley-piert	LC	(N)
Apium graveolens	Wild Celery	L	(N)
Aquilegia vulgaris	Columbine	L	(C)
Arabidopsis thaliana	Thale Cress	F	(N)
Arabis hirsuta	Hairy Rock-cress	L	(N)
Arctium minus	Lesser Burdock	C	(N)
Arenaria serpyllifolia	Thyme-leaved Sandwort	LC	(N)
Armeria maritima	Thrift	LC	(N)
Armoracia rusticana	Horse-radish	C	(N)
Artemisia absinthium	Wormwood	L	(N)
Arum maculatum	Lords-and-Ladies	C	(N)
Asparagus officinalis	Garden Asparagus	R	(N)
Asplenium adiantum-nigrum	Black Spleenwort	F	(N)
Asplenium ruta-muraria	Wall-rue	L	(N)
Asplenium trichomanes	Maidenhair Spleenwort	E	(N)
Aster aggregate	Michaelmas Daisy	L	(A)
Aster tripolium	Sea Aster	LC	(N)
Athyrium filix-femina	Lady Fern	LC	(N)
Atriplex glabriuscula	Babington's Orache	VL	(N)
Atriplex halimus	Shrubby Orache	L	(C)
Atriplex laciniata	Frosted Orache	R	(N)
Atriplex littoralis	Grass-leaved Orache	L	(N)
Atriplex patula	Common Orache	C	(N)
Atriplex portulacoides	Sea Purslane	LC	(N)
Atriplex prostrata	Spear-leaved Orache	LC	(N)
Avena fatua	Wild Oat	L	(C)
Ballota nigra	Black Whorehound	LC	(N)
Barbarea intermedia	Medium-flowered Winter-cress	L	(C)
Barbarea verna	American Winter-cress	VL	(E)
Barbarea vulgaris	Winter-cress	C	(N)
Bellis perennis	Daisy	VC	(N)
Beta vulgaris	Sea Beet	LC	(N)
Betula pendula	Silver Birch	F	(N)
Betula pubescens	Downy Birch	F	(N)
Bidens tripartita	Trifid Bur-marigold	LC	(N)
Blackstonia perfoliata	Yellow-wort	L	(N)
Bolboschoenus maritimus	Sea Club-rush	LC	(N)
Borago officinalis	Common Borage	L	(P)
Brachypodium sylvaticum	False Brome	VC	(N)
Brassica napus	Rape	LC	(C)
Bromopsis erecta	Upright Brome	LC	(N)
Bromopsis ramosa	Hairy Brome	LC	(N)
Bromus hordeaceus	Least Soft-brome	C	(N)
Bryonia dioica	White Bryony	LC	(N)
Buddleja davidii	Butterfly-bush	LC	(C)
Bupleurum tenuissimum	Slender Hare's-ear	L	(N)
Cakile maritima	Sea Rocket	VL	(N)
Calamagrostis epigejos	Wood Small-reed	L	(N)
Callitriche stagnalis	Common Water-starwort	F	(N)
Calluna vulgaris	Heather	LC	(N)
Calystegia sepium	Hedge Bindweed	C	(N)
Calystegia silvatica	Large Bindweed	LC	(E)
Calystegia soldanella	Sea Bindweed	VL	(N)
Capsella bursa-pastoris	Shepherd's-purse	C	(N)
Cardamine flexuosa	Wavy Bitter-cress	VC	(N)
Cardamine hirsuta	Hairy Bitter-cress	LC	(N)
Cardamine pratensis	Lady's Smock	C	(N)
Carduus crispus	Welted Thistle	LC	(N)
Carduus nutans	Musk Thistle	LC	(N)
Carduus tenuiflorus	Slender Thistle	L	(N)
Carex arenaria	Sand Sedge	L	(N)
Carex binervis	Green-ribbed Sedge	L	(N)
Carex distans	Distant Sedge	L	(N)
Carex disticha	Brown Sedge	L	(N)
Carex divisa	Divided Sedge	L	(N)
Carex divulsa	Grey Sedge	LC	(N)
Carex extensa	Long-bracted Sedge	R	(N)
Carex flacca	Glaucous Sedge	LC	(N)
Carex hirta	Hairy Sedge	LC	(N)
Carex laevigata	Smooth-stalked Sedge	L	(N)
Carex muricata	Prickly Sedge	L	(N)

Carex otrubae	False Fox-sedge	LC	(N)
Carex otrubae	False Fox-sedge	LC	(N)
Carex panicea	Carnation Sedge	LC	(N)
Carex pendula	Pendulous Sedge	LC	(N)
Carex pilulifera	Pill Sedge	LC	(N)
Carex punctata	Dotted Sedge	R	(N)
Carex remota	Remote Sedge	LC	(N)
Carex riparia	Greater Pond-sedge	LC	(N)
Carex viridula	Common Yellow-sedge	LC	(N)
Carlina vulgaris	Carline Thistle	L	(N)
Carpinus betulus	Hornbeam	F	(N)
Castanea sativa	Sweet Chestnut	LC	(A)
Catapodium marinum	Sea Fern-grass	LC	(N)
Centaurea nigra	Common Knapweed	C	(N)
Centaurea scabiosa	Greater Knapweed	LC	(N)
Centaurium erythraea	Common Centaury	LC	(N)
Centaurium pulchellum	Lesser Centaury	L	(N)
Centranthus ruber	Red Valerian	L	(E)
Cerastium diffusum	Sea Mouse-ear	LC	(N)
Cerastium fontanum	Common Mouse-ear	F	(N)
Cerastium glomeratum	Sticky Mouse-ear	C	(N)
Cerastium semidecandrum	Little Mouse-ear	LC	(N)
Ceratophyllum demersum	Rigid Hornwort	LC	(N)
Chaenorhinum minus	Small Toadflax	LC	(N)
Chaerophyllum temulum	Rough Chervil	C	(N)
Chamerion angustifolium	Rosebay Willowherb	C	(N)
Chelidonium majus	Greater Celandine	F	(N)
Chenopodium album	Fat-hen	VC	(N)
Chenopodium chenopodioides	Saltmarsh Goosefoot	E	(N)
Chenopodium ficifolium	Fig-leaved Goosefoot	F	(N)
Chenopodium murale	Nettle-leaved Goosefoot	R	(N)
Chenopodium polyspermum	Many-seeded Goosefoot	F	(N)
Chenopodium rubrum	Red Goosefoot	F	(N)
Chenopodium vulvaria	Stinking Goosefoot	E	(N)
Chrysanthemum segetum	Corn Marigold	L	(N)
Cichorium intybus	Chicory	F	(C)
Circaea lutetiana	Enchanter's-nightshade	C	(N)
Cirsium acaule	Dwarf Thistle	LC	(N)
Cirsium arvense	Creeping Thistle	VC	(N)
Cirsium palustre	Marsh Thistle	F	(N)
Cirsium vulgare	Spear Thistle	VC	(N)
Claytonia perfoliata	Spring Beauty	F	(C)
Clematis vitalba	Traveller's-joy	VC	(N)
Clinopodium ascendens	Common Calamint	VL	(N)
Clinopodium vulgare	Wild Basil	LC	(N)
Cochlearia anglica	English Scurvygrass	F	(N)
Cochlearia danica	Danish Scurvygrass	LC	(N)
Colutea arborescens	Bladder-senna	R	(P)
Conium maculatum	Hemlock	LC	(N)
Convallaria majalis	Lily-of-the-Valley	VL	(E)
Convolvulus arvensis	Field Bindweed	VC	(N)
Conyza canadensis	Canadian Fleabane	LC	(C)
Cornus sanguinea	Dogwood	F	(N)
Coronopus didymus	Lesser Swine-cress	LC	(C)
Coronopus squamatus	Common Swine-cress	LC	(N)
Cortaderia selloana	Pampas-grass	VR	(C)
Corylus avellana	Hazel	VC	(N)
Cotoneaster horizontalis	Wall Cotoneaster	L	(E)
Crambe maritima	Sea Kale	L	(N)
Crassula tillaea	Mossy Stonecrop	VL	(N)
Crataegus monogyna	Common Hawthorn	VC	(N)
Crepis capillaris	Smooth Hawk's-beard	C	(N)
Crepis vesicaria	Beaked Hawk's-beard	F	(E)
Crithmum maritimum	Rock Samphire	F	(N)
Cruciata laevipes	Crosswort	LC	(N)
Cuscuta epithymum	Common Dodder	LC	(N)

Cymbalaria muralis	Ivy-leaved Toadflax	F	(E)
Cynoglossum officinale	Hound's-tongue	F	(N)
Cynosurus cristatus	Crested Dog's-tail	C	(N)
Cynosurus echinatus	Rough Dog's-tail	VR	(N)
Cytisus scoparius	Broom	LC	(N)
Dactylis glomerata	Cock's-foot	VC	(N)
Dactylorhiza fuchsii	Common Spotted-orchid	LC	(N)
Dactylorhiza incarnata	Early Marsh-orchid	L	(N)
Danthonia decumbens	Heath Grass	LC	(N)
Daucus carota	Wild Carrot	C	(N)
Deschampsia cespitosa	Tufted Hair-grass	C	(N)
Deschampsia flexuosa	Wavy Hair-grass	LC	(N)
Dianthus armeria	Deptford Pink	E	(N)
Digitalis purpurea	Foxglove	LC	(N)
Digitaria sanguinalis	Hairy Finger-grass	VR	(C)
Diplotaxis muralis	Stinkweed	L	(A)
Diplotaxis tenuifolia	Wall Rocket	L	(N)
Dipsacus fullonum	Wild Teasel	C	(N)
Dryopteris dilatata	Common Buckler-Fern	C	(N)
Dryopteris filix-mas	Male Fern	VC	(N)
Echium vulgare	Viper's Bugloss	LC	(N)
Eleocharis palustris	Common Spike-rush	LC	(N)
Elodea canadensis	Canadian Waterweed	LC	(A)
Elodea nuttallii	Nuttall's Waterweed	LC	(A)
Elytrigia atherica	Sea Couch	C	(N)
Elytrigia juncea	Sand Couch	L	(N)
Elytrigia repens	Common Couch	C	(N)
Epilobium ciliatum	American Willowherb	C	(C)
Epilobium hirsutum	Great Willowherb	LC	(N)
Epilobium lanceolatum	Spear-leaved Willowherb	R	(N)
Epilobium montanum	Broad-leaved Willowherb	C	(N)
Epilobium obscurum	Short-fruited Willowherb	LC	(N)
Epilobium palustre	Marsh Willowherb	C	(N)
Epilobium parviflorum	Hoary Willowherb	LC	(N)
Epilobium tetragonum	Square-stalked Willowherb	LC	(N)
Equisetum arvense	Common Horsetail	LC	(N)
Equisetum fluviatile	Water Horsetail	F	(N)
Equisetum palustre	Marsh Horsetail	L	(N)
Equisetum telmateia	Great Horsetail	C	(N)
Erica cinerea	Bell Heather	LC	(N)
Erica tetralix	Cross-leaved Heath	LC	(N)
Erodium cicutarium	Common Stork's-bill	LC	(N)
Erodium moschatum	Musk Stork's-bill	VR	(N)
Erophila verna sens.lat.	Common Whitlowgrass	C	(N)
Erucastrum gallicum	Hairy Rocket	R	(C)
Eryngium maritimum	Sea Holly	VR	(N)
Erysimum cheiranthoides	Treacle Mustard	F	(C)
Erysimum cheiri	Wallflower	R	(A)
Euonymus europaeus	Spindle	LC	(N)
Eupatorium cannabinum	Hemp Agrimony	LC	(N)
Euphorbia amygdaloides	Wood Spurge	LC	(N)
Euphorbia exigua	Dwarf Spurge	LC	(N)
Euphorbia helioscopia	Sun Spurge	C	(N)
Euphorbia paralias	Sea Spurge	VR	(E)
Euphorbia peplus	Petty Spurge	C	(N)
Euphorbia portlandica	Portland Spurge	E	(N)
Euphrasia micrantha	Slender Heath-eyebright	R	(N)
Euphrasia officinalis	Eyebright aggregate	LC	(N)
Fagus sylvatica	Beech	VC	(N)
Fallopia convolvulus	Black Bindweed	C	(N)
Fallopia japonica	Japanese Knotweed	F	(E)
Festuca arundinacea	Tall Fescue	LC	(N)
Festuca brevipila	Hard Fescue	VR	(N)
Festuca filiformis	Fine-leaved Sheep's-fescue	LC	(N)
Festuca gigantea	Giant Fescue	LC	(N)

Festuca ovina agg.	Sheep's-fescue	LC	(N)	*Juncus gerardii*	Saltmarsh Rush	LC	(N)
Festuca pratensis	Meadow-fescue	LC	(N)	*Juncus inflexus*	Hard Rush	LC	(N)
Festuca rubra agg.	Red Fescue	C	(N)	*Juncus maritimus*	Sea Rush	LC	(N)
Filago minima	Small Cudweed	LC	(N)	*Kickxia elatine*	Sharp-leaved Fluellen	LC	(N)
Foeniculum vulgare	Fennel	LC	(C)	*Kickxia spuria*	Round-leaved Fluellen	F	(N)
Frankenia laevis	Sea-heath	VR	(N)	*Knautia arvensis*	Field Scabious	LC	(N)
Fraxinus excelsior	Ash	VC	(N)	*Lactuca serriola*	Prickly Lettuce	F	(N)
Fumaria muralis	Common Ramping-fumitory	F	(N)	*Lagurus ovatus*	Hare's-tail	VR	(E)
Fumaria officinalis	Common Fumitory	C	(N)	*Lamium album*	White Dead-nettle	C	(N)
Galeopsis tetrahit agg	Common Hemp-nettle	LC	(N)	*Lamium amplexicaule*	Henbit Dead-nettle	F	(N)
Galium aparine	Goose-grass	C	(N)	*Lamium purpureum*	Red Dead-nettle	C	(N)
Galium mollugo	Hedge Bedstraw	C	(N)	*Lapsana communis*	Nipplewort	VC	(N)
Galium palustre	Marsh Bedstraw	LC	(N)	*Lathyrus latifolius*	Broad-leaved Everlasting-pea	O	(C)
Galium saxatile	Heath Bedstraw	LC	(N)	*Lathyrus nissolia*	Grass Vetchling	L	(N)
Galium verum	Lady's Bedstraw	LC	(N)	*Lathyrus pratensis*	Meadow Vetchling	VC	(N)
Gastridium ventricosum	Nit-grass	VR	(N)	*Lavatera arborea*	Tree Mallow	VL	(N)
Genista tinctoria	Dyer's Greenweed	L	(N)	*Leontodon autumnalis*	Autumn Hawkbit	C	(N)
Gentianella amarella	Autumn Gentian	LC	(N)	*Leontodon hispidus*	Rough Hawkbit	LC	(N)
Geranium dissectum	Cut-leaved Crane's-bill	VC	(N)	*Leontodon saxatilis*	Lesser Hawkbit	LC	(N)
Geranium lucidum	Shining Crane's-bill	VL	(N)	*Lepidium campestre*	Field Pepperwort	L	(N)
Geranium molle	Dove's-foot Crane's-bill	VC	(N)	*Lepidium draba*	Hoary Cress	LC	(C)
Geranium purpureum	Little Robin	R	(N)	*Lepidium heterophyllum*	Smith's Cress	F	(N)
Geranium pusillum	Small-flowered Crane's-bill	F	(N)	*Lepidium ruderale*	Narrow-leaved Pepperwort	F	(N)
Geranium pyrenaicum	Hedgerow Crane's-bill	LC	(N)	*Leucanthemum vulgare*	Oxeye Daisy	C	(N)
Geranium robertianum	Herb Robert	VC	(N)	*Leymus arenarius*	Lyme-grass	VL	(N)
Geranium rotundifolium	Round-leaved Crane's-bill	R	(N)	*Ligustrum ovalifolium*	Garden Privet	O	(A)
Geum urbanum	Herb Bennet	VC	(N)	*Ligustrum vulgare*	Wild Privet	LC	(N)
Glaucium flavum	Yellow Horned-poppy	L	(N)	*Limonium humile*	Lax Sea-lavender	R	(N)
Glaux maritima	Sea Milkwort	L	(N)	*Limonium vulgare*	Common Sea-lavender	LC	(N)
Glechoma hederacea	Ground Ivy	VC	(N)	*Limonium x neumanii*	Hybrid Sea-lavender	VR	(N)
Gnaphalium uliginosum	Marsh Cudweed	LC	(N)	*Linaria purpurea*	Purple Toadflax	F	(C)
Hedera helix	Ivy	VC	(N)	*Linaria repens*	PaleToadflax	VL	(N)
Helictotrichon pratense	Meadow Oat-grass	F	(N)	*Linaria vulgaris*	Common Toadflax	C	(N)
Heracleum sphondylium	Hogweed	VC	(N)	*Linum bienne*	Pale Flax	R	(N)
Hesperis matronalis	Dame's-violet	L	(N)	*Linum catharticum*	Fairy Flax	LC	(N)
Hieracium aggregate	Hawkweed	C	(N)	*Linum usitatissimum*	Cultivated Flax	O	(C)
Hippophae rhamnoides	Sea-buckthorn	O	(P)	*Listera ovata*	Common Twayblade	LC	(N)
Hirschfeldia incana	Hoary Mustard	L	(C)	*Lobularia maritima*	Sweet Alison	VL	(C)
Holcus lanatus	Yorkshire Fog	VC	(N)	*Lolium multiflorum*	Italian Rye-grass	C	(A)
Honckenya peploides	Sea Sandwort	F	(N)	*Lolium perenne*	Perennial Rye-grass	VC	(N)
Hordeum jubatum	Foxtail Barley	VR	(C)	*Lonicera periclymenum*	Honeysuckle	C	(N)
Hordeum marinum	Sea Barley	VR	(N)	*Lotus corniculatus*	Common Bird's-foot-trefoil	C	(N)
Hordeum murinum	Wall Barley	LC	(N)	*Lotus glaber*	Narrow-leaved Bird's-foot-trefoil		
Hordeum secalinum	Meadow Barley	F	(N)	*Lotus pedunculatus*	Greater Bird's-foot-trefoil	LC	(N)
Humulus lupulus	Hop	LC	(N)	*Lunaria annua*	Honesty	O	(C)
Hyacinthoides non-scripta	Bluebell	C	(N)	*Lupinus arboreus*	Tree Lupin	F	(E)
Hydrocotyle vulgaris	Marsh Pennywort	LC	(N)	*Luzula campestris*	Field Wood-rush	LC	(N)
Hypericum humifusum	Trailing St John's-wort	LC	(N)	*Luzula multiflora*	Heath Wood-rush	LC	(N)
Hypericum perforatum	Common St John's-wort	VC	(N)	*Lychnis coronaria*	Rose Campion	R	(E)
Hypericum pulchrum	Slender St. John's-wort	LC	(N)	*Lychnis flos-cuculi*	Ragged Robin	LC	(N)
Hypericum tetrapterum	Square-stalked St.John's-wort	LC	(N)	*Lycium barbarum*	Duke of Argyll's Teaplant	O	(C)
Hypochaeris glabra	Smooth Cat's-ear	R	(N)	*Lycopus europaeus*	Gipsywort	LC	(N)
Hypochaeris radicata	Common Cat's-ear	LC	(N)	*Lysimachia nummularia*	Creeping Jenny	LC	(N)
Ilex aquifolium	Holly	VC	(N)	*Lysimachia punctata*	Dotted Loosestrife	L	(E)
Inula crithmoides	Golden Samphire	LC	(N)	*Lysimachia vulgaris*	Yellow Loosestrife	C	(N)
Iris foetidissima	Stinking Iris	L	(N)	*Malus domestica*	Apple	F	(S)
Iris pseudacorus	Yellow Flag	LC	(N)	*Malva moschata*	Musk Mallow	C	(N)
Jasione montana	Sheep's-bit	LC	(N)	*Malva neglecta*	Dwarf Mallow	F	(N)
Juncus acutus	Sharp Rush	VR	(N)	*Malva sylvestris*	Common Mallow	C	(N)
Juncus ambiguus	Frog Rush	VL	(N)	*Matricaria discoidea*	Pineapple Weed	VC	(C)
Juncus articulatus	Jointed Rush	LC	(N)	*Matricaria recutita*	Scented Mayweed	LC	(N)
Juncus bufonius	Toad Rush	LC	(N)	*Medicago arabica*	Spotted Medick	F	(N)
Juncus bulbosus	Bulbous Rush	LC	(N)	*Medicago lupulina*	Black Medick	VC	(N)
Juncus conglomeratus	Compact Rush	LC	(N)	*Medicago polymorpha*	Toothed Medick	R	(N)
Juncus effusus	Soft Rush	LC	(N)				

Medicago sativa	Lucerne Aggregate	F	(N)	Phleum pratense	Timothy	C	(N)
Melilotus albus	White Melliot	F	(C)	Phragmites australis	Common Reed	C	(N)
Melilotus altissimus	Golden Melliot	F	(C)	Phyllitis scolopendrium	Hart's-tongue	F	(N)
Melilotus indicus	Small Melliot	R	(C)	Picris echioides	Bristly Oxtongue	LC	(N)
Melilotus officinalis	Ribbed Melliot	F	(C)	Picris hieracioides	Hawkweed Oxtongue	LC	(N)
Mentha aquatica	Water Mint	C	(N)	Pilosella officinarum	Mouse-ear Hawkweed	LC	(N)
Mentha arvensis	Corn Mint	LC	(N)	Pimpinella saxifraga	Burnet-saxifrage	LC	(N)
Mentha spicata	Spear Mint	F	(C)	Pinus nigra	Black Pine	O	(P)
Mentha x villosa	Large Apple-mint	O	(C)	Pinus sylvestris	Scots Pine	LC	(N)
Mercurialis annua	Annual Mercury	LC	(C)	Plantago coronopus	Buck's-horn Plantain	LC	(N)
Milium effusum	Wood Millet	LC	(N)	Plantago lanceolata	Ribwort Plantain	VC	(N)
Mimulus guttatus	Monkeyflower	L	(N)	Plantago major	Greater Plantain	VC	(N)
Moehringia trinervia	Three-nerved Sandwort	C	(N)	Plantago maritima	Sea Plantain	LC	(N)
Moenchia erecta	Upright Chickweed	L	(N)	Poa annua	Annual Meadow-grass	VC	(N)
Molinia caerulea	Purple Moor-grass	LC	(N)	Poa bulbosa	Bulbous Meadow-grass	VR	(N)
Montia fontana	Blinks	LC	(N)	Poa humilis	Spreading Meadow-grass	L	(N)
Myosotis arvensis	Common Forget-me-not	C	(N)	Poa infirma	Early Meadow-grass	C	(N)
Myosotis discolor	Changing Forget-me-not	F	(N)	Poa pratensis sens.str	Smooth Meadow-grass	VC	(N)
Myosotis ramosissima	Early Forget-me-not	L	(N)	Poa trivialis	Rough Meadow-grass	VC	(N)
Myosotis sylvatica	Wood Forget-me-not	VL	(C)	Polygala serpyllifolia	Heath Milkwort	LC	(N)
Myosurus minimus	Mousetail	R	(N)	Polygala vulgaris	Common Milkwort	LC	(N)
Myriophyllum spicatum	Spiked Water-milfoil	F	(N)	Polygonum arenastrum	Equal-leaved Knotgrass	L	(N)
Narcissus aggregate	Cultivated Daffodil	F	(C)	Polygonum aviculare	Knotgrass	C	(N)
Nuphar lutea	Yellow Water-lily	F	(N)	Polygonum maritimum	Sea Knotgrass	VR	(N)
Nymphaea alba	White Water-lily	L	(N)	Polygonum oxyspermum	Ray's Knotgrass	R	(N)
Odontites vernus	Red Bartsia	LC	(N)	Polypodium interjectum	Polypody		(N)
Oenanthe crocata	Hemlock Water-dropwort	VC	(N)	Polypodium vulgare	Polypody		(N)
Oenanthe lachenalii	Parsley Water-dropwort	VL	(N)	Polystichum setiferum	Soft Shield-fern	LC	(N)
Oenanthe pimpinelloides	Corky-fruited Water-dropwort	LC	(N)	Populus alba	White Poplar	L	(A)
Oenothera aggregate	Evening-primrose agg.	F	(E)	Populus nigra 'Italica'	Lombardy Poplar	LC	(P)
Oenothera biennis	Common Evening-primrose	F	(E)	Populus tremula	Aspen	LC	(N)
Oenothera cambrica	Small-flowered Evening-primrose	R	(E)	Populus x canadensis	Poplar	O	(A)
Oenothera glazioviana	Large Evening-primrose	LC	(C)	Populus x canescens	Grey Poplar	F	(P)
Ononis repens	Common Restharrow	LC	(N)	Potamogeton pectinatus	Fennel-leaved Pondweed	LC	(N)
Ononis spinosa	Spiny Restharrow	VL	(N)	Potentilla anglica	Trailing Tormentil	L	(N)
Onopordum acanthium	Cotton Thistle	VL	(C)	Potentilla anserina	Silverweed	VC	(N)
Ophrys apifera	Bee Orchid	F	(N)	Potentilla argentea	Hoary Cinquefoil	R	(N)
Orchis morio	Green-winged Orchid	LC	(N)	Potentilla erecta	Tormentil	LC	(N)
Origanum vulgare	Marjoram	LC	(N)	Potentilla reptans	Creeping Cinquefoil	VC	(N)
Ornithopus perpusillus	Bird's-foot	LC	(N)	Primula vulgaris	Primrose	C	(N)
Orobanche minor	Common Broomrape	F	(N)	Prunella vulgaris	Selfheal	VC	(N)
Osmunda regalis	Royal Fern	VL	(N)	Prunus avium	Wild Cherry	LC	(N)
Otanthus maritimus	Cottonweed	E	(N)	Prunus cerasifera	Cherry Plum	F	(P)
Oxalis acetosella	Wood Sorrel	LC	(N)	Prunus domestica	Wild Plum	F	(A)
Oxalis articulata	Pink Oxalis	L	(E)	Prunus domestica ssp.	Bullace	O	(A)
Papaver dubium ssp. dubium	Long-headed Poppy	LC	(N)	Prunus spinosa	Blackthorn	VC	(N)
Papaver dubium ssp. lecoqii	Yellow-juiced Poppy	R	(N)	Pseudofumaria lutea	Yellow Corydalis	O	(E)
Papaver rhoeas	Corn Poppy	F	(N)	Pteridium aquilinum	Bracken	VC	(N)
Papaver somniferum	Opium Poppy	F	(C)	Puccinellia distans	Reflexed Saltmarsh-grass	L	(N)
Parapholis incurva	Curved Hard-grass	R	(N)	Puccinellia fasciculata	Borrer's Saltmarsh-grass	L	(N)
Parapholis strigosa	Sea Hard-grass	L	(N)	Puccinellia maritima	Common Saltmarsh-grass	F	(N)
Pastinaca sativa	Parsnip	LC	(N)	Puccinellia rupestris	Stiff Saltmarsh-grass	L	(N)
Pedicularis sylvatica	Lousewort	LC	(N)	Pulicaria dysenterica	Common Fleabane	VC	(N)
Pentaglottis sempervirens	Green Alkanet	O	(E)	Quercus cerris	Turkey Oak	LC	(A)
Persicaria amphibia	Amphibious Bistort	LC	(N)	Quercus ilex	Holm Oak	O	(A)
Persicaria hydropiper	Water Pepper	LC	(N)	Quercus robur	Pedunculate Oak	VC	(N)
Persicaria lapathifolia	Pale Persicaria	LC	(N)	Radiola linoides	Allseed	L	(N)
Persicaria maculosa	Redshank	C	(N)	Ranunculus acris	Meadow Buttercup	VC	(N)
Petasites fragrans	Winter Heliotrope	F	(E)	Ranunculus arvensis	Corn Buttercup	R	(N)
Petrorhagia nanteuilii	Childing Pink	VR	(N)	Ranunculus bulbosus	Bulbous Buttercup	C	(N)
Petroselinum segetum	Corn Parsley	R	(C)	Ranunculus circinatus	Fan-leaved Water-crowfoot	VR	(N)
Phalaris arundinacea	Reed Canary-grass	C	(N)	Ranunculus ficaria	Lesser Celandine	VC	(N)
Phalaris canariensis	Canary-grass	LC	(C)	Ranunculus flammula	Lesser Spearwort	LC	(N)
Phleum arenarium	Sand Cat's-tail	VR	(N)	Ranunculus hederaceus	Ivy-leaved Crowfoot	L	(N)
Phleum bertolonii	Small Cat's-tail	LC	(N)	Ranunculus peltatus	Pond Water-crowfoot	LC	(N)

Scientific name	Common name		
Ranunculus repens	Creeping Buttercup	VC	(N)
Ranunculus sardous	Hairy Buttercup	VR	(N)
Ranunculus sceleratus	Celery-leaved Buttercup	F	(N)
Ranunculus trichophyllus	Three-leaved Water-crowfoot	R	(N)
Raphanus raphanistrum			
ssp. *maritimus*	Sea Radish	VL	(N)
Raphanus raphanistrum			
ssp. *raphanistrum*	Wild Radish	C	(C)
Reseda lutea	Wild Mignonette	C	(N)
Reseda luteola	Weld	LC	(N)
Rhinanthus minor	Yellow Rattle	LC	(N)
Rhododendron ponticum	Rhododendron	LC	(E)
Ribes rubrum	Red Currant	LC	(N)
Ribes sanguineum	Flowering Currant	O	(C)
Ribes uva-crispa	Gooseberry	LC	(C)
Rorippa microphylla	Narrow-fruited Water-cress	L	(N)
Rorippa sylvestris	Creeping Yellow-cress	F	(N)
Rosa arvensis	Field Rose	C	(N)
Rosa canina agg.	Dog Rose	VC	(N)
Rosa micrantha	Small-flowered		
	Sweet-briar	LC	(N)
Rosa obtusifolia	Round-leaved Dog-rose	F	(N)
Rosa pimpinellifolia	Burnet Rose	VL	(N)
Rosa rubiginosa	Sweet Briar	O	(N)
Rosa stylosa	Short-styled Field-rose	F	(N)
Rubus caesius	Dewberry	LC	(N)
Rubus fruticosus agg.	Bramble	VC	(N)
Rubus idaeus	Raspberry	C	(N)
Rumex acetosa	Sheep's Sorrel	LC	(N)
Rumex acetosella	Common Sorrel	VC	(N)
Rumex conglomeratus	Clustered Dock	LC	(N)
Rumex crispus	Curled Dock	VC	(N)
Rumex obtusifolius	Broad-leaved Dock	VC	(N)
Rumex pulcher	Fiddle-leaved Dock	L	(N)
Rumex sanguineus	Wood Dock	C	(N)
Ruppia cirrhosa	Spiral Tassel-weed	VR	(N)
Ruppia maritima	Beaked Tassel-weed	R	(N)
Ruscus aculeatus	Butcher's-broom	LC	(N)
Sagina apetala			
ssp. *apetala*	Annual Pearlwort	LC	(N)
Sagina apetala ssp. *erecta*	Upright Pearlwort	C	(N)
Sagina maritima	Sea Pearlwort	L	(N)
Sagina procumbens	Mossy Pearlwort	VC	(N)
Sagina subulata	Heath Pearlwort	F	(N)
Salicornia aggregate	Glasswort	R	(N)
Salicornia dolichostachya	Long-spiked Glasswort	F	(N)
Salicornia europaea	Common Glasswort	R	(N)
Salicornia fragilis	Yellow Glasswort	VL	(N)
Salicornia nitens	Shiny Glasswort	VR	(N)
Salicornia obscura	Glaucus Glasswort	VR	(N)
Salicornia pusilla	One-flowered Glasswort	VL	(N)
Salicornia pusilla			
x *ramosissima*	Hybrid Glasswort	VR	(N)
Salicornia ramosissima	Purple Glasswort	LC	(N)
Salix alba	White Willow	LC	(N)
Salix caprea	Goat Willow	C	(N)
Salix cinerea			
ssp. *oleifolia*	Grey Willow	F	(N)
Salix fragilis	Crack Willow	C	(N)
Salix repens	Creeping Willow	LC	(N)
Salix viminalis	Osier	LC	(N)
Salsola kali ssp. *kali*	Saltwort	VR	(N)
Salvia verbenaca	Clary	R	(N)
Sambucus nigra	Common Elder	VC	(N)
Sanguisorba minor	Salad Burnet	LC	(N)
Saponaria officinalis	Soapwort	L	(E)
Sarcocornia perennis	Perennial Glasswort	F	(N)
Schoenoplectus lacustris	Common Club-rush	F	(N)
Scrophularia auriculata	Water Figwort	LC	(N)
Scrophularia nodosa	Common Figwort	C	(N)
Scutellaria minor	Lesser Skullcap	LC	(N)
Sedum acre	Biting Stonecrop	F	(N)
Sedum album	White Stonecrop	VL	(E)
Sedum anglicum	Sea Stonecrop	LC	(N)
Senecio aquaticus	Marsh Ragwort	LC	(N)
Senecio erucifolius	Hoary Ragwort	LC	(N)
Senecio jacobaea	Common Ragwort	VC	(N)
Senecio squalidus	Oxford Ragwort	LC	(C)
Senecio sylvaticus	Heath Groundsel	LC	(N)
Senecio viscosus	Sticky Groundsel	F	(N)
Senecio vulgaris	Groundsel	VC	(N)
Serratula tinctoria	Saw-wort	E	(N)
Seriphidium maritimum	Sea Wormwood	L	(N)
Sherardia arvensis	Field Madder	LC	(N)
Silaum silaus	Pepper-saxifrage	LC	(N)
Silene dioica	Red Campion	LC	(N)
Silene latifolia	White Campion	C	(N)
Silene nutans	Nottingham Catchfly	VR	(N)
Silene uniflora	Sea Campion	F	(N)
Silene vulgaris	Bladder Campion	L	(N)
Silybum marianum	Milk Thistle	R	(E)
Sinapis alba	White Mustard	F	(C)
Sinapis arvensis	Charlock	VC	(N)
Sison amomum	Stone Parsley	LC	(N)
Sisymbrium officinale	Hedge Mustard	VC	(C)
Sisymbrium orientale	Eastern Rocket	VL	(N)
Smyrnium olusatrum	Alexanders	F	(E)
Solanum dulcamara	Bittersweet	VC	(N)
Solanum nigrum	Black Nightshade	LC	(N)
Solidago canadensis	Garden Goldenrod	L	(C)
Solidago virgaurea	Goldenrod	LC	(N)
Sonchus arvensis	Corn Sow-thistle	LC	(N)
Sonchus asper	Prickly Sow-thistle	C	(N)
Sonchus oleraceus	Smooth Sow-thistle	LC	(N)
Sorbus aria	White Beam	LC	(E)
Sorbus aucuparia	Rowan	LC	(C)
Sorbus intermedia	Swedish Whitebeam	O	(C)
Spartina anglica	Common Cord-grass	LC	(N)
Spartina maritima	Small Cord-grass	R	(N)
Spartina x townsendii	Townsends Cord-grass	VR	(N)
Spartium junceum	Spanish Broom	O	(P)
Spergula arvensis	Corn Spurrey	C	(N)
Spergularia marina	Lesser Sea-spurrey	LC	(N)
Spergularia media	Greater Sea-spurrey	LC	(N)
Spergularia rubra	Sand Spurrey	LC	(N)
Spiranthes spiralis	Autumn Lady's-tresses	L	(N)
Stachys officinalis	Betony	LC	(N)
Stachys palustris	Marsh Woundwort	LC	(N)
Stachys sylvatica	Hedge Woundwort	VC	(N)
Stachys x ambigua	Hybrid Woundwort	O	(N)
Stellaria graminea	Lesser Stitchwort	C	(N)
Stellaria holostea	Greater Stitchwort	VC	(N)
Stellaria media	Common Chickweed	VC	(N)
Stellaria pallida	Lesser Chickweed	VL	(N)
Suaeda maritima	Annual Seablite	LC	(N)
Succisa pratensis	Devil's-bit Scabious	LC	(N)
Symphytum officinale	Common Comfrey	LC	(N)
Symphytum orientale	White Comfrey	R	(C)
Symphytum x uplandicum	Russian Comfrey	LC	(C)
Tamarix gallica	Tamarisk	L	(A)

Tamus communis	Black Bryony	C	(N)
Tanacetum parthenium	Feverfew	F	(C)
Tanacetum vulgare	Tansy	F	(N)
Taraxacum aggregate	Dandelion	VC	(N)
Taxus baccata	Yew	C	(N)
Teesdalia nudicaulis	Shepherd's Cress	VL	(N)
Teucrium scorodonia	Wood Sage	LC	(N)
Thlaspi arvense	Common Penny-cress	LC	(N)
Thymus polytrichus	Wild Thyme	LC	(N)
Thymus pulegioides	Large Thyme	L	(N)
Tilia x europaea	Lime	F	(P)
Torilis japonica	Upright Hedge-parsley	C	(N)
Tragopogon pratensis	Goat's-beard	LC	(N)
Trifolium arvense	Hare's-foot Clover	LC	(N)
Trifolium campestre	Hop Trefoil	C	(N)
Trifolium dubium	Lesser Trefoil	VC	(N)
Trifolium fragiferum	Strawberry Clover	L	(N)
Trifolium hybridum	Alsike Clover	C	(C)
Trifolium medium	Zigzag Clover	F	(N)
Trifolium micranthum	Slender Trefoil	LC	(N)
Trifolium ornithopodioides	Bird's-foot Clover	LC	(N)
Trifolium pratense	Red Clover	VC	(N)
Trifolium repens	White Clover	VC	(N)
Trifolium scabrum	Rough Clover	VL	(N)
Trifolium striatum	Knotted Clover	LC	(N)
Trifolium subterraneum	Subterranean Clover	LC	(N)
Trifolium suffocatum	Suffocated Clover	R	(N)
Triglochin maritimum	Sea Arrowgrass	LC	(N)
Tripleurospermum inodorum	Scentless Mayweed	VC	(N)
Tripleurospermum maritimum	Sea Mayweed	LC	(N)
Trisetum flavescens	Yellow Oat-grass	LC	(N)
Tussilago farfara	Colt's-foot	C	(N)
Typha angustifolia	Lesser Bulrush	L	(N)
Typha latifolia	Greater Reedmace	LC	(N)
Ulex europaeus	Gorse	LC	(N)
Ulex gallii	Western Gorse	VR	(N)
Ulex minor	Dwarf Gorse	LC	(N)
Ulmus aggregate	Elm	C	(N)
Ulmus glabra	Wych Elm	LC	(E)
Ulmus procera	English Elm	C	(N)
Ulmus x vegeta	Huntington Elm	VR	(E)
Urtica dioica	Stinging Nettle	VC	(N)
Urtica urens	Small Nettle	LC	(N)
Valeriana officinalis	Common Valerian	LC	(N)
Valerianella carinata	Keeled-fruited Cornsalad	R	(N)
Valerianella locusta	Common Cornsalad	F	(N)
Valerianella rimosa	Broad-fruited Cornsalad	VR	(N)
Verbascum blattaria	Moth Mullein	R	(C)
Verbascum nigrum	Dark Mullein	LC	(N)
Verbascum thapsus	Common Mullein	LC	(N)
Verbascum virgatum	Twiggy Mullein	VR	(N)
Verbena officinalis	Vervain	LC	(N)
Veronica agrestis	Green Field-speedwell	O	(N)
Veronica arvensis	Wall Speedwell	C	(N)
Veronica chamaedrys	Germander Speedwell	VC	(N)
Veronica filiformis	Slender Speedwell	F	(A)
Veronica hederifolia	Ivy-leaved Speedwell	LC	(N)
Veronica montana	Wood Speedwell	LC	(N)
Veronica officinalis	Heath Speedwell	LC	(N)
Veronica persica	Common Field-speedwell	C	(C)
Veronica polita	Grey Field-speedwell	F	(N)
Veronica serpyllifolia	Thyme-leaved Speedwell	LC	(N)
Viburnum lantana	Wayfaring-tree	LC	(P)
Viburnum opulus	Guelder Rose	C	(P)
Vicia cracca	Tufted Vetch	VC	(N)
Vicia hirsuta	Hairy Tare	C	(N)
Vicia lathyroides	Spring Vetch	VL	(N)
Vicia sativa	Common Vetch	C	(N)
Vicia sepium	Bush Vetch	C	(N)
Vicia tetrasperma	Smooth Tare	LC	(N)
Vinca major	Greater Periwinkle	L	(E)
Viola arvensis	Field Pansy	C	(N)
Viola canina	Heath Dog-violet	L	(N)
Viola lactea	Pale Dog-violet	VL	(N)
Viola odorata	Sweet Violet	LC	(N)
Viola reichenbachiana	Early Dog-violet	LC	(N)
Viola riviniana	Common Dog-violet	VC	(N)
Viola tricolor	Wild Pansy	R	(C)
Vulpia bromoides	Squirreltail Fescue	LC	(N)
Vulpia ciliata	Bearded Fescue	R	(N)
Vulpia fasciculata	Dune Fescue	VR	(N)
Zostera angustifolia	Narrow-leaved Eelgrass	LC	(N)
Zostera marina	Common Eelgrass	R	(N)
Zostera noltii	Dwarf Eelgrass	LC	(N)

Bird's-foot-trefoil

References

Allen, M & Gardiner, J 'Unveiling Langstone Harbour' (*Current Archaeology* No 69).

Barrett, J & Younge, C M (1958) *Collins Pocket Guide to the Sea Shore*, Collins.

Brewis, A, Bowman P, Rose F (1996) *The Flora of Hampshire*, Harley Books.

Brown, R, (1983) *The Story of Hayling Island*, Milestone Publications.

Clarke, JM & Eyre, JA (1993) *Birds of Hampshire*, Hamphire Ornithological Society.

Cook, R (1996) *Britain in old Photographs, Havant and Hayling Island*, Sutton.

Dony, JG, Jury, SL & Perring, FH (1986) *English Names of Wildflowers*, BSBI.

Garrard, I & Streeter, D (1983) *The Wild Flowers of the British Isles*, Macmillan.

Gibbons, B& L (1988) *Creating a Wildlife Garden*, Hamlyn.

Goater, B (1974) *The Butterflies and Moths of Hampshire and the Isle of Wight*, E.W Classey.

Hammond, N, & Pearson, B (1994) *Waders, Hamlyn Bird Behaviour Guides*, Hamlyn.

Mabey, R (1996) *Flora Britannica*, Sinclair Stevenson.

Marshall, JA & Haes, ECM (1988) *Grasshoppers and Allied Insects of Great Britain and Ireland*, Harley Books.

Oates, M, Taverner, J & Green, D (2000) *The Butterflies of Hampshire*, Pisces Publications.

Powell, D (1999) *A Guide to the Dragonflies of Great Britain*, Arlequin Press.

Prater, AJ (1981) *Estuary Birds of Britain and Ireland*, Poyser.

Pycroft, N (1998) *Hayling - An Island of Laughter and Tears*, Self Published.

Reger, J (1996) *Chichester Harbour- A History*, Phillimore.

Skelton, I (1826) *Topographical and Historical Account of Hayling Island*.

Skinner, B (1984) *Colour Identification Guide to the Moths of the British Isles*, Viking.

Snow DW & Perrins CM (1998) *The Birds of the Western Palearctic, Concise Edition*, O.U.P.

Thomas, FGS (1978) *The King Holds Hayling* (Concise Edition), Pelham.

Thomas, J & Lewington, R (1991) *The Butterflies of Britain & Ireland*, Dorling Kindersley.

Tubbs, C (1999) *The Ecology, Conservation and History of the Solent*, Packman.

Tweed, R (1999) *A History of Langstone Harbour and its environs in the County of Hampshire*, Dido Publications.

Wigginton, MJ (1999) *British Red Data Books 1 Vascular plants*, JNCC.

Yalden, D (1999) *The History of British Mammals*, Poyser.

Goldeneye

Acknowledgements

We would like to thank and acknowledge the following for their help and assistance during the preparation of this book.

All those private landowners on Hayling who gave permission to enter their land. Havant Borough Council and Dave Archer at the Beachlands office for information and the loan of aerial photographs. Noel and Valerie Pycroft for cups of tea and long chats when they happily shared their unrivalled knowledge of the island. Chris Palmer and the staff at the Havant Museum. George Else for his useful suggestions on bees. John Phillips for his comments on moths. Pete Gammage and Tim Lawman for their comments on the bird list. James McCallum for information on Brent Geese. John Badley for his useful comments. Pete Smithers for information on the *Argiope* spider. Ralph Hollins for his numerous helpful comments. Dennis Johnson and Simon Colenutt for allowing us to use their excellent photographs. Pat Holt at the Hayling Islander for the picture of the swamp cat. Pete Selby for his sterling efforts in drawing up the flora list for the island and the members of the BSBI for their diligent plant recording. Dr Francis Rose for his foreword, expertise and encouragement.

Colleagues in the Hampshire County Council Countryside Service, especially Andy Parfitt, Dave Ball, Ian Livermore and Jim Hobson.

Roger Mann, Matthew Cooper and Colin Markham at Wotton Printers for their expertise during the production of this book.

A very large thank you to Aimee Phillips, Beatrice Gillam, John Durnell, Joyce Greenwood, and Michael Walters for their tireless work in editing the text.

Pete Durnell and John Walters *March 2001*

Useful Addresses

The Royal Society for the Protection of Birds
The Lodge, Sandy
Bedfordshire SG19 2DL

RSPB South East Regional Office
Tel 01273 463642

Hampshire Ornithological Society (HOS)
Membership Secretary
John Norton
36 Penhale Gardens
Fareham
Hants PO14 4NL

Hampshire County Council (HCC)
Countryside Service
South Eastern Office
Staunton Country Park
Middle Park Way
Havant PO9 5HB.
Tel 023 92 476411

Havant Borough Council (HBC)
Leisure & Community Services
Civic Offices
Havant
Hampshire PO9 2AX
Tel 023 92 474174
HBC Environmental Officer, Hayling Oysterbeds
Tel 023 92 446378

Hampshire Wildlife Trust (HWT)
Woodside House, Woodside Road
Eastleigh, Hampshire SO50 4ET.
Tel 023 80 613636

Butterfly Conservation
Hampshire Branch
Jenny Mallett
Great Funtley Farm, Titchfield Lane
Wickham, Hampshire PO15 6EA
Tel 01329 832177

Langstone Harbour Board
The Harbour Office
Ferry Road
Hayling Island
Environmental Officer
Tel 023 92 463419

Chichester Harbour Conservancy
The Harbour Office
Itchenor, West Sussex PO20 7AW
Tel 01243 512301

British Trust for Ornithology (BTO)
The Nunnery
Thetford, Norfolk IP24 2PU
Tel 01842 750050

Species Index Mainly refers to where species are first mentioned and highlighted in bold.

133